CHRIST'S HEALING POWER TODAY

Other books by Peter Gammons

BATTLE STATIONS
BELIEVING IS SEEING
ALL PREACHERS GREAT AND SMALL
A TOUCH FROM HEAVEN
THE ANOINTING
THE MISSING INGREDIENT
SOWING AND REAPING
THE JONAH COMPLEX
THE RETURN OF JESUS CHRIST

CHRIST'S HEALING POWER TODAY

PETER GAMMONS

MONARCH
Tunbridge Wells

Unless otherwise indicated, biblical quotations are from the
Revised Authorised Version

ISBN 1 85424 151 6

British Library Cataloguing-in-Publication Data.
A catalogue record for this book is available
from the British Library.

Production and Printing in England for
MONARCH PUBLICATIONS
Owl Lodge, Langton Road, Speldhurst, Tunbridge Wells,
Kent TN3 0NP by
Nuprint Ltd, Station Road, Harpenden, Herts AL5 4SE

THIS BOOK is written with the earnest prayer that many thousands may learn to appropriate the blessings of God's Word.

Special thanks to Sarah Cheeseman, Carolyn Brown and Carolyn Anderson for typing and re-typing this manuscript and to Pat Darwood, Dave Evans, Michael Fenton-Jones and Derek Minto for their editorial assistance.

CONTENTS

FOREWORD BY DEREK BOND

It is my privilege to write a short foreword to this remarkable book.

Having travelled and ministered with Peter since 1978 I have seen his ministry grow and flourish. I have seen him step out in faith and achieve wonderful things through God, while some of us are still standing at the starting block wondering which way we should run. Peter is a true fighter in God's army!

During the fifteen years that we have worked together, Peter has preached to over sixty million people worldwide. I have seen him minister to and pray for tens of thousands of people. God has opened the doors for him to share Christ with Presidents, Prime Ministers and world leaders. Yet, although he has spoken to so many, he has never lost his compassion for people. He is driven by a longing to take Christ's saving and healing power to this needy world of ours. I remember seeing Peter in floods of tears as he prayed for an old man with multiple sclerosis. The next day we received a call to say that this man had been healed.

His heart and fervour for God's Word and his ability to communicate Christ and encourage faith is always refreshing.

Peter is not only a writer, nor just a preacher: he is a good friend and a loyal servant of God.

Rev Derek Bond

FOREWORD BY ANDREW KETTLE

I have accompanied Peter across the Philippines and have witnessed amazing signs and wonders; the blind receiving their sight, limbs being restored, deaf ears opened and many people giving their lives to Jesus.

The most amazing miracles took place among the pagan mountain people of Bontoc. Over half of the population of Bontoc gave their lives to Jesus and on the last night we lost count of how many blind received their sight (I know of at least four). Many deaf were healed. Again I lost count of how many cripples discarded their sticks and canes. I have never seen anything like this before.

As the crusade service started the skies lit up. At first I wondered if we were going to have thunder, but no, it was as if it was a sign from the Lord that a breakthrough had happened in the heavenlies, as the principalities and powers that have ruled here were defeated.

The Anglican Bishop came to see me after the crusade absolutely amazed at what had happened. He had never seen anything like it in his life and he is an elderly man. He kept thanking Peter for coming.

Many Christians in the West find it hard to believe in miracles, but we saw these things with our own eyes. I count it a privilege to write a foreword to this book and to endorse the accounts of the miracles recorded in it.

Rev Andrew Kettle
Missionary

PART ONE
KNOWING GOD'S WILL CONCERNING HEALING

1 GOD'S HEALING WORD

Those who are in truth His disciples, receiving grace from Him, do in His Name perform miracles, so as to promote the welfare of other men, according to the gift which each one has received from Him. For some do certainly and truly drive out devils, so that those who have thus been cleansed from evil spirits frequently both believe [in Christ], and join themselves to the Church. Others have foreknowledge of things to come; they see visions, and utter prophetic expressions. Others still, heal the sick by laying their hands upon them, and they are made whole. Yea, moreover, as I have said, the dead even have been raised up and remained among us for many years.

Iranaeus AD 140-203
Against Heresies Book 2

> 'My son, give attention to My Words; incline your ear to My sayings. Do not let them depart from your eyes; keep them in the midst of your heart; for they are life to those who find them, and health to all their flesh.' Proverbs 4:20–22

Despite the fact that the Bible is packed with positive promises revealing God's will concerning healing, many Christians are unaware of them and therefore are full of doubt–even unbelief–when they pray.

A foundation for our faith, built firmly on the Word of God, is vital for receiving healing or any other blessing from the Lord. That is why I have written the following chapters, packed with scripture and biblical teaching on the subject.

Our faith must stand firmly on the promises of God. May I encourage you to read these truths over and over again to build your faith to combat the doubts of the enemy.

I have found that those who pray, but fail to receive the miracle from Christ that they desire, often lack knowledge of what the Bible says about God's blessings and healing, for without knowing these truths we have no basis for our faith.

Most church members have at some time been taught that sickness is God's blessing in disguise, that it may teach them humility and patience, and that it may have a divine purpose and therefore should not be resisted, but graciously accepted and humbly borne with patience for God's glory. Yet I have also discovered that very few of those people can quote scriptures in the Bible that promise physical healing, even though there are many.

If these promises are not taught the people cannot know them. If people do not know these truths, there can be no faith for miracles. If there is no faith for miracles, they will not be experienced.

As believers, we need to decide that God's Word will always be the final authority for us.

Jesus said that the Word of God is the seed. The only way to stop Satan stealing it from us is to stand firm on God's Word as our Lord did...'It is written!' Right from the time when man first sinned in the Garden of Eden, Satan has been out to make people doubt God's Word:

> Now the serpent was more cunning than any beast of the field which the Lord God had made. And he said to the woman, 'Has God indeed said, "You shall not eat from every tree of the garden?"...you shall not die.'
> Genesis 3:1,4

You must realise that Satan's only power to defeat you is if he can deceive you into doubting God's Word. It is the oldest trick in the Book. He tried it on Adam and Eve and tricked them with the words, 'Has God said?'

He tried to put doubt in our Lord's mind, after His baptism, concerning God's Word and His identity. The Father spoke from heaven, saying, 'This is my beloved Son in

Whom I am well pleased.' Almost immediately Satan came along saying, 'If you are the Son of God...' Our Lord would not be moved. He declared, 'It is written...' Jesus stood firmly on the Word of God, as we must.

The devil always tries to sow doubt over anything that God has done. Did he not try to make you doubt your salvation? The only way that we can counter doubt is with the Word of God. The Bible says that if I confess my sins, God is faithful and just to forgive me my sins and to cleanse me from all unrighteousness (1 John 1:9). I have confessed them, so I am forgiven. It tells me that if I open the door of my life to Jesus, He WILL come in (Revelation 3:20). It tells me that if I believe on the Lord Jesus Christ I WILL be saved (Acts 2:21).

The same principle is true when it comes to healing. If we do not have a sound biblical foundation, knowing the promises of God concerning healing, we will waver and doubt our healing in the same way that we would doubt God's forgiveness if we did not have a good foundation in the Word of God.

Since I learned to stand on God's Word I have never doubted God has forgiven me. I did not say that I have always felt saved. Our feelings change and are very unpredictable. That is why our faith must be based on the unchanging promises of God's Word and not on how we feel.

Read over and over the chapters in this section, which are full of biblical truths on healing until you have a good foundation in the Word of God to combat all the doubts of the enemy. The Word of God is the only means of deliverance from doubt.

Throughout the Old and New Testament we see God healing the sick. As we will see together, the Scriptures reveal God as 'The Lord Who heals you'. He does not change, neither does His attitude towards sin, sickness and disease.

If we hope to see miracles and experience healing we must realise that it does not just happen to people automatically, any more than salvation just happens to people. God does not force blessings onto us; they are received by faith. Although it is 'by grace' that we are saved, it is 'through faith' (Ephesians 2:8).

If a preacher faithfully preaches salvation, then people will get saved. If he faithfully preaches the promise of the Holy Spirit, then people will also be filled with the Spirit. The same is true of healing. It is only as healing is preached that people start to get healed. It does not matter how much a pastor prays for the sick in church, if he does not preach faith for healing, then it is unlikely that anyone will get healed.

One of the major problems is that for years preachers taught that God does not heal the sick today. This has led to a 'spirit' or 'atmosphere' of unbelief in the church. If a minister preached in his church that Jesus does not forgive sin and that salvation is by good works, how many would get saved? Only preaching the truth of the Gospel will lead to people being saved. Only by preaching the truth of God's Word concerning healing can we break this stronghold of unbelief.

Have you ever tried witnessing to someone who has been brought up to believe that salvation is by good works? Despite the Scriptural teaching to the contrary, years of false teaching have often led to a hardness towards gospel truths. The only hope is that the person will re-consider what they have 'always believed' in the light of God's Word. The same is true for Christians. For many years believers have heard that God does not heal the sick today and that miracles have ceased. Consequently, even when they know that this cannot be true, because God does not change and even though they may know of people who have been healed, they still fight unbelief.

It may be that I will write some things which are different from what another preacher, pastor or Bible teacher has taught you. However, the only relevant question must be not, 'What have we heard others teach about healing?' or 'What does Peter Gammons say?' but, 'What does the Bible say?' God's Word must be the final authority for us.

How often have we seen that traditional, long-held views die hard? Yet Jesus warned us that the traditions of men can make the Word of God 'of no effect'. If we exalt the views of man above the Word of God we must expect to receive nothing from God.

Many Christians have never studied God's Word on this important subject for themselves. Others have a theology of healing based on the experience of other Christians. Some assume that, because many fine Christians have not been healed, it is not God's Will. Others think that, because someone else was healed that they will also be healed. Yet to build our faith on the experiences of someone else, whether their experience was positive or negative, instead of building on the Word of God, is to build on sand.

If our own experience does not match-up to the Word of God, it is our experience that must change, not God's Word! To have faith we must accept what God's Word says, even if it conflicts with everything we have ever believed before.

Why is there a lack of miracles in many circles today? The Bible says: 'Faith comes by hearing and hearing by the Word of God' (Romans 10:17). Yet, too often, faith has left us after hearing the words of others.

Ministers may call for a month of fasting but this will not bring the miraculous into evidence if we do not teach the promises of God in their absolute simplicity. We can call for entire nights of prayer, but it will be of no avail if our teaching does not encourage simple faith in Christ.

We need to see that the Word of God is His voice. It has the same authority as if He were speaking to us in person. When you read the Bible remember that you are having a personal conversation with the Lord.

The absolute integrity of God's written Word is the only basis for consistent faith. We should give God's Word the same place as we would give Christ if He were physically in our presence.

We cannot separate God from His Word. The promises we read in the Bible are God speaking to us personally. They are just as much ours as a cheque that is drawn on a bank and which is made out to us. Faith means that we expect God to do what He has promised. That is why faith comes by hearing the Word of God. You must know what God has promised to do before you can expect Him to do it.

God need not give any special revelation of His will when He has plainly given His revealed will in His Word. God's Word is His will. God's promises reveal His will. When we read of what He promises to do, we then know what it is His will to do.

The Bible is the only way that we can know God's will, for God's Word never changes. As the psalmist put it, 'Forever O Lord, Your Word is settled in heaven' (Psalm 119:89).

> God is not a man, that He should lie, nor a son of man that He should repent. Has He said it and will He not do it? Or has He spoken and will not make it good? Numbers 23:19

Jesus said:

> 'Heaven and earth will pass away, but my Word will by no means pass away.' Matthew 24:35

The issue must be not what do we believe about healing but what God's Word says on the subject for we can only receive from God on His terms. Most of us have had to do a lot of re-thinking on this subject.

Faith for healing

> Faith comes by hearing, and hearing by the Word of God. Romans 10:17

God's Word is packed with positive promises so that our faith is firm and unshakeable.

Some people say, 'I wish I had faith like yours for healing,' as though faith is a commodity which just drops out of the sky. There is only one way that we can obtain faith and that is by reading and believing in the absolute integrity of God's Word. The same Word that brings us faith to receive forgiveness also brings us faith to receive healing. The same Word that reveals God's will concerning healing also brings us the faith to receive our healing.

God has told us:

> My son, attend to My Words; incline your ear to My sayings. Let them not depart from your eyes; keep them in the midst of your heart. These are life to those that find them and health to all their flesh. Proverbs 4:20–22

We will only discover the blessings that are ours in Christ by 'attending to' the Word of God, by a constant, diligent, prayerful study of it. We must feed on His Word until it becomes a part of us.

Jesus said:

> 'If you abide in Me, and My words abide in you, you will ask what you desire, and it shall be done for you.'
> John 15:7

As we 'abide in' or 'live in' the Word of God, faith comes so that we can pray expectantly. It is only by God's Word that doubts go and faith comes.

God tells us that we must have faith. Now if God demanded that we have faith when it is impossible for us to have faith, then we could challenge His justice. But if He places within our hands the means whereby faith can be produced, then the responsibility rests with us whether or not we have faith. He has provided the way whereby everyone can have faith–and He has told us exactly how to receive faith.

Some Christians say, 'If only I had a Word from heaven about healing.' We do; it is called the Bible. The Bible is the source of faith. To say, 'I wish I had more faith' is like sitting outside a garage saying, 'I wish I had more petrol.' We must go to the source and fill up. The responsibility is with us. God, by giving us His Word, has already done His part.

Unbelief can hold back God moving in your life

What natural food is to the physical man, the Word of God is to the spiritual man. It produces faith. There is no other way. In Matthew 13:58 we read that at Nazareth, 'He did not do many mighty works there because of their unbelief.' Just as unbelief kept Christ from healing the sick then, it will surely do so today.

Mark records how unbelief limited God's moving in Jesus' own home town: 'He could do no mighty deeds there, except that He laid His hands on a few sick people and healed them. And He marvelled because of their unbelief' (Mark 6:5,6).

Isn't it astonishing that there are things that the Son of God 'could not do'? That is what God's Word says. If a preacher had said that, he would have been accused of being a heretic. But it is the Word of God that says it. Our unbelief can hinder God. Do not misunderstand me, God can, of course, do anything. He is sovereign. But in His sovereignty He has chosen to work in response to faith. As a sovereign God He has every right to do that.

Years of preaching that God does not perform miracles today or that we cannot expect Him to work miracles for us, has left an atmosphere of unbelief in our land which so often stops our prayers breaking through. The Word of God is clear. Jesus' miracles were not just the intervention of a sovereign God doing whatever He liked. He responded to faith. Faith is vital to receiving answered prayer (Mark 11:24, Matthew 21:21, Mark 9:23, Matthew 9:29).

When Jesus' disciples asked why they had been unable to cast the demon out of a child, Jesus said, 'Because of your unbelief' (Matthew 17:20).

Mark 9:17–27 tells us of a father who brought his demon-possessed son to the Lord and said, 'If thou canst do anything, have compassion on us, and help us.' Jesus replied, 'If thou canst believe, all things are possible to him that believeth.' Christ said in effect to this father, 'The "if" does not lie with Me, but with you.'

It is a waste of time praying for healing to 'see if it works'. The Bible tells us to 'ask in faith, with no doubting, for he who doubts is like a wave of the sea, driven and tossed by the wind. For let not that man suppose that he will receive anything from the Lord' (James 1:6,7). The book of James tells us that it is 'the prayer of faith that saves the sick and the Lord will raise him up' (James 5:15).

It is the 'prayer of faith' and not just prayer. It is vital that we grasp this if we hope to see miracles.

The day of miracles is past for those who believe that it is, for Jesus said, 'According to your faith let it be to you' (Matthew 9:29). Signs only follow 'them that believe' (Mark 16:16–20).

It is my prayer that we may come to God's Word afresh and that faith will come to your heart.

2 CREATION AND COVENANT TO CHRIST

How often it has happened, and still does that devils have been driven out in the name of Christ; also, by calling on His Name and prayer, that the sick have been healed.

Martin Luther
Letters of Spiritual Counsel

AN OVERVIEW OF CREATION

Sickness was never God's intention. God created the world according to His perfect will. There was no sin or disease in the Garden of Eden.

God created man and woman perfect physically, mentally and spiritually. Eden was a place of happiness, tranquillity and abundance. That was God's plan for all mankind.

The fall

When Adam sinned, sickness and disease entered the world. God had promised that the day in which he disobeyed, he would 'die' and it happened. When Adam sinned, instantly he died spiritually and also he began to die physically. Death and decay began their evil course (Genesis 2:17). The inference of the original text is 'in dying thou shalt die', suggesting a process of death had begun.

Adam did not instantly die physically, in fact he lived another 930 years, but from this time onwards people's life-span began to decrease.

God had created men and women to have dominion, but as a result of their disobedience, physical and spiritual death, along with sickness, entered the world. 'Wherefore, as by one man sin entered into the world, and death by sin and so death passed upon all men, for all have sinned' (Romans 5:12 AV).

Physical death and all that produces it are the direct results of sin in the world. Do not misunderstand me; I am not saying that all sickness is the result of the individual's sin. Much sickness is just the result of our living in a fallen world.

Let me give you an example. If a person chain smokes, he may well die of lung cancer. However, there may be another person who does not smoke, but works in an office where everyone else smokes. He too may die from inhaling the smoke of his colleagues. In a similar way, some are sick because of their own sin, but for most it is just the result of living in the sinful environment of our world.

Sickness is a fact of life which most of us have come to terms with. But what many do not realise is that God offers us healing.

HEALING AND THE OLD COVENANT

Healing is not just a New Testament blessing. Right back in the book of Genesis, God healed the barrenness of Abimelech's wife and her servants in answer to Abraham's prayer.

> So Abraham prayed to God; and God healed Abimelech, his wife, and his maidservants. Then they bore children. Genesis 20:17

The Lord heard Hezekiah's prayer and healed him too.

> Thus says the Lord, the God of David your father; 'I have heard your prayer, I have seen your tears; surely I

> will heal you. On the third day you shall go up to the house of the Lord.' 2 Kings 20:5

God revealed himself to Israel as 'Yahweh Rapha', meaning, 'I am the Lord who heals you' Exodus 15:26. Throughout the Old and New Testaments, we discover that our God is a healing God. He has not changed. One translation of this verse is, 'I am the Lord that heals you. I am a healer by nature.'

The nature of God is to heal. He is still Yahweh Rapha today–'The Lord that heals', for 'with Him is no variation' (James 1:17), literally, 'He does not change even slightly.'

Even under the Old Covenant, God promised that, if Israel kept His Word, He would 'take sickness away from the midst of them' (Exodus 23:25,26).

> 'You shall serve the Lord your God, and He will bless your bread and water. And *I will take sickness away from the midst of you.* No one shall suffer miscarriage or be barren in your land; I will fulfil the number of your days.' Exodus 23:25,26

In Exodus 15:26 we read:

> 'If thou wilt diligently hearken to the voice of the Lord thy God, and wilt do that which is right in His sight, and wilt give ear to His commandments, and keep all His statutes, I will put none of these diseases upon thee, which I have brought upon the Egyptians: for *I am the Lord that healeth thee.*'

He promised to protect His people from disease and to remove all sickness from their midst, if they would walk in obedience.

> 'The Lord will take away from you *all sickness,* and will afflict you with none of the terrible diseases of Egypt which you have known, but will lay them on all those who hate you.' Deuteronomy 7:15

This blessing of health covered them from birth to old age; God promised them healing, health and long life.

Throughout Israel's history we find them in sickness and in pestilence turning to God in repentance and confession; and always, when their sins were forgiven, their sicknesses were healed. Once, when Israel sinned and spoke against God, fiery serpents entered their camp, and many died from the snake bites.

> Therefore the people came to Moses, and said, 'We have sinned, for we have spoken against the Lord and against you; pray to the Lord that He take away the serpents from us.' So Moses prayed for the people. Then the Lord said to Moses, 'Make a fiery serpent, and set it on a pole; and it shall be that everyone who is bitten, when he looks at it, shall live.' So Moses made a bronze serpent, and put it on a pole; and so it was, if a serpent had bitten anyone, when he looked at the bronze serpent, he lived. Numbers 21:7–9

Though to the Hebrew mind, it was God who struck them, it is interesting that the sickness was from the serpents, always a type, a model or a picture of Satan's activities in the Bible. The Hebrew words are 'the serpents, the seraphim's'.

God healed those who were bitten by fiery serpents as they looked at a brazen serpent on a pole. This we later discover was a type (a picture or model) of Calvary (John 3:14,15). If everyone who looked at the brazen serpent was healed then, it is logical that everyone who looks to Jesus can be healed today.

The brazen serpent was a picture of how Christ would take on Himself the sin of the world, that all who looked to Him might be made whole. Christ would be made sin for us, assuming the vile and dishonoured name of sinful man, as if He were indeed the worst of sinners, even though He Himself was sinless. For us He took the sting from sickness, Satan, sin and death.

Jesus said, 'As Moses lifted up the serpent in the wilderness, even so must the Son of Man be lifted up' (John 3:14,15). When the people cried to God, He heard their cry and provided a remedy–the serpent lifted up. Those who cry to God today discover that God has heard their cry and has provided for them a remedy–Christ lifted up. The remedy was for everyone that was bitten then. The remedy is for whoever believes today.

In their remedy they received both forgiveness for their sins and healing for their bodies. In Christ, we receive forgiveness for our sins and healing for our sick bodies today.

A careful study of the Scriptures clearly shows that God is both the Saviour and Healer of His people. There were no exceptions then; their remedy was for everyone that is bitten, just as our remedy is for whoever believes. Everyone was commanded to look individually at the remedy then. Everyone is commanded to believe individually on Christ today. Since their curse was removed by the lifting up of the type of Christ, our curse was certainly removed by Christ Himself being lifted up.

The type or picture of Christ could not mean more to those Israelites then than Christ means to us today. Surely we can receive today, through Christ Himself, all of the blessings that they received through the type of Christ.

God revealed Himself as both the one 'Who forgives all your iniquities; who heals all your diseases' (Psalm 103:3). We cannot be faithful to the Word of God and preach one without the other.

Throughout Israel's wilderness experience, God provided for all of their material needs, healing for the babies and deliverance from their enemies. The Bible tells us that not one person from among their tribes was sick or feeble. Can you imagine that?

> He also brought them out with silver and gold, and there was *none feeble* among his tribes. Psalm 105:37

As believers, we accept so much of the world's way of thinking. We often live in less than God's people lived in under the Old Covenant! Don't accept the reasoning that 'getting old' means that you have to become feeble. We read of God's people on their wilderness journey, that not one of them was feeble. That included all the old people and all the small children!

Don't just accept all the aches and pains that the enemy puts on you as an inevitable part of growing older. God can renew your youth (Isaiah 40:31).

As I write these words, I am staying in the home of a ninety-year-old man, who still drives his car, and walks about freely and unaided. He has had two major healings in answer to the prayer of faith in the last couple of years. When he is sick, he still believes to get healed.

Do not misunderstand me. I am not saying that everyone can live until he is ninety! Rather, that while we are still alive God can continue to heal and give life to our bodies.

In Romans 8:11 (AV), Paul writes:

> But if the spirit of Him that raised up Jesus from the dead dwells in you, He that raised up Christ from the dead shall also quicken your mortal bodies by His Spirit that dwelleth in you.

The verb 'shall quicken' is *zóopoiéssei*, the future third person singular of *zóopoiéo*, and comes from *zóé*, 'life', and *poieó*, 'I make'. This bringing to life (quickening) is not at the Resurrection.

The word *thanétos* (mortal) does not mean dead but 'liable to or subject to death'. The Greek word for a dead human body is *nekros*, but never *thanétos*, which always refers to something 'subject to death', never to a dead body.

Paul wrote in Romans 6:12, 'Let not sin reign in your mortal (*thanétos*, the same word as in Romans 8:11) body'. Had Paul said, 'Let not sin reign in your dead body', it would not have made sense.

John Calvin, that superb Greek scholar, was right when he says of Romans 8:11, 'The quickening of the mortal body here cannot refer to the resurrection of the saints, but must mean a giving of life to their bodies, while here upon earth, through the Spirit.'

One day we will receive resurrection bodies that are no longer subject to decay. However, while we are still alive, God can 'quicken them'.

Some people have said, 'If we are not sick, how can we die?' Yet who said that we have to leave this life via the path of sickness and pain? When God calls your spirit home, can you not just go to be with Him? Many a precious Saint has gone home this way.

F.F. Bosworth, the author of *Christ the Healer*, announced one day when in his 80s, 'This is the greatest day of my life. God has shown me that I am going home.' Then he called in a friend for a time of fellowship and went to be with his Lord.

I recently heard the lovely story of a Methodist lady in her 90s. She testified that 40 years earlier she had accepted Jesus, not only as her Saviour, but also as her Physician. She hadn't been sick at all during the time since. The day she went to be with the Lord, at 94, she announced at the breakfast table, 'I'm going home this morning' and asked for a reading by her family from the Scriptures. Then she said, 'There's Jesus, I must go! Good-bye' and went to be with the Lord, sitting in her favourite chair!

I know that this is an ideal way of dying that not all experience, yet I write these things, not to bring any condemnation on those who are sick, but to lift your faith. We do not have to resign ourselves to sickness, aches and pains. Many Christians just give in to all the circumstances of life. It is time to fight back in faith.

The Bible seems to encourage us that, as we walk in faith and obedience, we should believe that we will have long and healthy lives.

> 'You shall walk in all the ways which the Lord your God has commanded you, that you may live and that it may be well with you, and that you may *prolong your days* in the land you shall possess.' Deuteronomy 5:33

> 'Do not be excessively wicked, nor be foolish; why should you *die before your time*?' Ecclesiastes 7:17

> 'My son, do not forget my law, but let your heart keep my commands; for *length of days and long life* and peace they will add to you.' Proverbs 3:1,2

> 'Honour your father and your mother, that your *days may be long* upon the land which the Lord your God is giving you.' Exodus 20:12
>
> 'So if you walk in My ways, to keep My statutes and My commandments, as your father David walked, then I will *lengthen your days.*' 1 Kings 3:14
>
> 'The fear of the Lord *prolongs days,* but the years of the wicked will be shortened.' Proverbs 10:27
>
> 'You shall serve the Lord your God, and He will bless your bread and water. And I will take sickness away from the midst of you. No-one shall suffer miscarriage or be barren in your land; *I will fulfil the number of your days.*' Exodus 23:25,26[1]

Again we see an ideal that we can believe for. The Word of God reveals so many blessings and truths that we have been unaware of. Many Christians are fearful of praying for healing in case they are praying against God's will, but we should not be afraid. It is only when our prayer of faith is not answered as we had believed, that we have to trust that God knows best.

So we see that sickness was never God's intention but when Adam sinned, sickness and disease entered the world. Although sickness is a fact of life which most of us have come to terms with, even back in the book of Genesis, God offered healing. He revealed Himself to Israel as 'The Lord who heals you' and demonstrated that it was His nature to heal and to restore. Even under the Old Covenant, God promised that as His people walked in obedience He would 'take sickness away from the midst of them'.

'I am the Lord who heals you' (Exodus 15:26) was God's healing promise. It was not man's idea. God established a statute of healing for His people as they walked in obedience. Nowhere in the Bible is it even implied that this statute of divine healing has been revoked. Rather, God says, 'I am the Lord, I do not change' (Malachi 3:6).

God has never changed His mind concerning healing.

Having seen how healing was available to all of Israel, are

we suggesting that God's people enjoyed a better covenant than we have today? Never! Because of the redemptive work of Christ, we have a better covenant established upon better promises (Hebrews 8:6)!

So, was healing available to Israel under the Old Covenant, to those under the law, but not to us under grace? In the next chapter we will see how the New Testament reveals even more wonderful truths concerning God's healing power and His desire to make us whole.

NOTE

[1] See also Deuteronomy 4:40; 5:16; 6:2; Psalm 91:16.

3 God's Will Revealed in Jesus

Instead of the ministry of healing diverting from the more significant matter of salvation for the soul, we have seen more conversions in a single week, than we ever saw in a whole year of evangelistic work during the thirteen years before the Lord led us to preach this part of the gospel in a bolder and more public way.

F. F. Bosworth, *Christ the Healer*
p Fleming H. Revell Books;
used with permission

In the beginning was the Word and the Word was with God, and the Word was God...The Word became flesh and dwelt among us. John 1:1,14a

One of the great truths of Christianity is that Jesus is God incarnate. God became man. Jesus came to show us God's love and care for a hurting, broken world. He came to show us God's desire to heal and to restore.

If we want to know God's will concerning healing we must look at Jesus. If you want to know what God's Word says about healing, look at Jesus. He is God's Word on the subject. He is the Word of God made flesh. He said, 'I do not seek My own will but the will of the Father who sent me' (John 5:30).

If we want to know God's will concerning healing we should carefully look at Jesus' life, for He is the exact image of the Father and only did the things which His Father told Him. He said, 'I and My Father are one' (John 10:30) and that to know Him was to know the Father (John 8:19). If you have ever doubted God's will concerning healing, look at Jesus. He came to show us what God is like. Jesus said, 'He who has seen Me, has seen the Father' (John 14:9). His earthly walk was a demonstration of God's perfect will.

In the Old Testament God revealed Himself as the Lord who heals (Exodus 15:26). Jesus further demonstrated God's desire to heal and said that it is Satan who is out to kill, to steal and to destroy (John 10:10).

In the book of Job (regarded by many as the oldest book of the Bible), we see that it was Satan who struck Job with boils (Job 2:7). We get the very first glimpse of who is behind the spread of sickness here.

> Then Satan went out from the presence of the Lord, and struck Job with painful boils from the sole of his foot to the crown of his head. Job 2:7

The Hebrew mind saw God as sovereign and ultimately behind everything. Therefore on occasions the Old Testament text implies that God causes certain things which, rather, He permits. Understanding this is very important. For example, in Exodus 15:26 we read:

> 'If you diligently heed the voice of the Lord your God and do what is right in His sight, I will put none of the diseases on you which I have brought on the Egyptians. For I am the Lord that heals you.'

In a similar way, some versions translate Isaiah 45:7 as:

> 'I form the light and create darkness, I make peace and create evil. I the Lord do all these things.'

Yet we know that God does not create evil. Evil does not proceed from God. Though He permits evil, He does not initiate it, nor does He cause sickness. Dr Robert Young, the author of *Young's Analytical Concordance to the Bible*, an outstanding Hebrew and Greek scholar, states in his book *Hints and Helps of Biblical Interpretation*, that in Exodus 15:26 the literal Hebrew reads, 'I will permit to be put upon thee none of the diseases which I have permitted to be brought upon the Egyptians, for I am the Lord that healeth thee.'

It is here that we see the mis-translation in some versions of the Bible. The permissive verb in the Hebrew has been translated in the active sense. We must not be confused between permission and commission. God permits people to steal and kill, but He certainly does not commission it. There is a vast difference between what God allows and what God actively causes.

In the New Testament God was glorified, not by people being sick but when they were healed. When the miraculous power of Christ is manifested today in the healing of the sick, thousands of souls believe on Christ as their Saviour, just as they did in Bible days.

> Believers were increasingly added to the Lord, multitudes of both men and women. So that they brought the sick out into the streets and laid them on beds, and couches...and they were all healed. Acts 5:14–16

Dr Luke, the author of the Book of Acts, also spoke of the source of sickness. In Acts 10:38 he wrote:

> God anointed Jesus of Nazareth with the Holy Spirit and with power, who went about doing good and healing all who were oppressed by the devil, for God was with Him. Acts 10:38

Luke calls sickness an oppression of the devil. He makes it clear that Satan was the source of sickness and not God.

> The Son of God was manifested that He might destroy the works of the devil. 1 John 3:8

Sickness is part of Satan's works. Christ, in His earthly ministry, always treated sin, disease and evil in the same way; He rebuked them all. He was made manifest to destroy them all.

Jesus said, 'The Son of Man is not come to destroy

people's lives, but to save them.' Sickness destroys. Christ came to save us (Greek: *sozo*, meaning 'to deliver us', 'to save and preserve us', 'to heal us', 'to give us life', 'to make us whole'). The devil is a liar and the slanderer who has propagated the idea that it is God who puts sickness on people.

It is amazing how many Christians have failed to see that Jesus demonstrated the Father's will. They seem to have the strange view that God put sickness on people and then Jesus went around taking it off them!

Jesus said that, 'The thief (speaking of Satan) does not come except to steal, and to kill, and to destroy; I have come that they may have life, and that they may have it more abundantly' (John 10:10).

The devil hates you. He wants to steal your faith, your love, your hope, your trust in God, your health, your earning power and your expectation of miracles. You name anything good in your life and it's the devil's business to try to steal it. This is the devil's sole purpose. He does not know anything else. When you feel robbed, cheated, pulled down, and depressed–that's the thief's work. The thief is trying to rob you of your life.

How often do we hear people say:

'Why me, God?'
'Why did I get sick?'
'Why did this go wrong?'
'Why don't I have enough money to pay my bills?'
'Why did God do that?'

You can tie yourself up in knots with the question 'Why?' However, you will never get an answer until you begin to understand some things about God; namely that He is good and on the side of health and that there is a devil who is bad and is out to destroy you and everything good in your life.

Blaming God will destroy your spiritual life and stop you ever recovering. It's time to ask God to forgive you for blaming Him and to start putting the blame where it belongs! It is time, in faith, to start fighting back!

In England we have a dilemma. Most people believe in

God and when you look at the glory of creation around us it is hard not to. The problem is that most people do not believe in the devil, so when anything goes wrong, they blame God. We see the extreme of this in insurance companies calling disasters 'an act of God.' Many preachers have continued to propagate this wrong concept and to slander God.

Jesus spent around two-thirds of His ministry healing the sick. He had no doubts where sickness came from. In Luke 13:11 we read, 'And, behold, there was a woman who had a spirit of infirmity eighteen years, and was bent over, and could in no way raise herself up.' Jesus said:

> '*Ought* not this woman, being a daughter of Abraham, whom *Satan has bound,* think of it, for eighteen years, be loosed from this bond on the Sabbath day?' Luke 13:16

Firstly, Jesus saw her sickness as a bondage of Satan. He said, 'Satan has bound' her.

Secondly, He said, 'Ought not this woman whom Satan has bound...be loosed?' This is more than a statement of the Lord's willingness to heal. The word 'ought' expresses much more than willingness. It expresses something which it would be wrong not to do! It emphasises Divine healing as not only a possibility but as His normal provision.

Notice the words 'who had a spirit of infirmity'. The word for 'infirmity' here is *asteneia*, the commonest word in the Greek language for 'sickness'. This poor woman had been dominated for eighteen years by a spirit, here called 'a spirit of sickness'. Satan has 'spirits of sickness', whose one great work in this world is to propagate sickness and disease, to make people sick.

In Mark 9:25 we find that Satan also has 'deaf and dumb' spirits:

> When Jesus saw that the people came running together, He rebuked the unclean spirit, saying to him 'You deaf and dumb spirit, I command you, come out of him, and enter him no more.'

This may be different from what you have heard taught by teachers before, but notice that it **is** what the Bible says.

We can see that Satan was the cause behind this sickness, because Christ uses the same harsh word *epitimao* to rebuke sickness.

In Luke 4:35 we read, 'And Jesus rebuked *(epetimesen)* him (the evil spirit in the man), saying, "Be quiet, and come out of him" '. In Luke 4:39 we read, 'So He stood over her (Simon's wife's mother), and rebuked (*epetimesen*, the same word as in Luke 4:35) the fever, and it left her'.

So many Christians have been programmed sheepishly to pray, 'If it be Your will, Lord, heal me.' We need to see that in the gospels and the Book of Acts, Jesus and the early Church did not question God's will in this matter and neither did they pray passively for the sick. They told the sickness to leave or the lame person to get up and walk, the blind to see and the deaf to hear. They were not fearful of praying against God's will, for they knew that God had not made the person sick. Speaking the Word in faith is not demanding God to do something; He did not make them sick in the first place! We are telling the devil to release them in Jesus' Name.

We need to realise that Jesus healed **all** who came to Him in faith. I cannot find **one** person that He turned away unhealed. Surely this clearly demonstrates God's perfect will? If, as some have preached, sickness glorifies God, then Jesus must have robbed God of a lot of glory! Jesus then authorised His disciples to do the same, to preach, to heal the sick and to cast out demons (Matthew 10:7,8).

At no time did Jesus tell them to just preach and to stop healing the sick. The preaching of the gospel is incomplete without healing the sick. I firmly believe that just to preach and not to minister to the sick is a man-ordained act and not a biblical directive.

The Pharisees and religious leaders opposed Christ's healing in Bible days and there are still some around today who will do the same. Yet, in the same commission that Jesus has given the believer to 'preach the gospel to every creature', He has told us to 'lay hands on the sick and they will recover' (Mark 16:15–20).

Who are we to decide which of Jesus' commands we will obey?

Some have written off miracles and healing as 'side issues'. Yet, Jesus spent a major part of His ministry healing the sick and setting the captives free. To call such things 'side issues' is to imply that Jesus must have got very side-tracked in his ministry.

To question the importance of miracles is to question a major part of Christ's ministry and the Word of God. Jesus came both 'preaching and showing the glad tidings of the Kingdom of God' (Luke 8:1). He said, 'As the Father has sent Me, I also send you' (John 20:21).

We are called to walk in the same power, anointing and ministry as Jesus, to continue what He began. To pray or to speak in Jesus' Name, means to pray or to speak on His behalf, with His delegated authority.

Jesus told us to pray that God's will be done on earth as it is in heaven (Matthew 6:9,10) and the Word of God is clear that there is no sickness in heaven (Revelation 21:4).

Jesus said:

> 'If you then, being evil, know how to give good gifts to your children, how much more will your Father, who is in heaven give good things to those who ask Him?'
> Matthew 7:11

God is a good God. If you had children, would it be your will that your children were sick and afflicted? Would it be your will that they go through life poverty-stricken and in need? No. Then do you think a loving God wants that for His children?

Would you not be angry if someone accused your earthly father of some terrible deed which he did not do? How much more should we be righteously angry when our Heavenly Father is blamed for what Satan puts on people. God is a good God. Throughout the gospels we see the Lord taking sickness and disease from people, not putting it on them! He has not changed.

Nowhere in the teaching or practice of Jesus did He promote sickness. Nowhere did He counsel anyone that it was inevitable or profitable. Let us get back to the Bible! Nowhere did Jesus inflict sickness on anyone to accomplish some higher good, though He healed many people for that reason.

Nowhere in Scripture do we find Jesus encouraging people to 'accept their sickness as a gift from God' or 'to bear it for His glory', as many do today. Nowhere do we find Jesus exalting 'the finer qualities' that can be developed through illness. Jesus never met sickness passively. He never regarded sickness as a friend to be welcomed, but as an enemy to be defeated. Jesus saw sickness as oppression by the devil.

The faith of many who seek healing from Christ is hindered by the idea that God may have some purpose in their suffering, that perhaps their sickness has been put on them by God and that they should have patience and not pray for healing. Thousands of good people suffer for years, never daring to pray the prayer of faith.

In order to clear our minds of these teachings we need to understand that sickness is from Satan and not from God, that Satan has put it on us, not God.

Grasping these truths is **vital** if we hope to be healed.

> 'Bless the Lord, O my soul, and forget not all His benefits: Who forgives all your iniquities, who heals all your diseases.' Psalm 103:2,3

Even though healing is one of the benefits that God's Word tells us not to forget, it is one of the benefits which many in the Church have forgotten.

Notice that the Psalmist says that the Lord heals 'all of our diseases'. The word 'all' means that none is left out. The word 'all' means 'without exception'. As Spurgeon once put it, ' "all" means "all", not "all but the one you have got".'

If I preached that God would only forgive some sins, I would soon be branded as a heretic, for 'the blood of Jesus cleanses us from all sin' (1 John 1:7). Yet the same verse that assures us that God forgives 'all your iniquities', also tells us that He 'heals all your diseases' (Psalm 103:2,3). Who are we to treat the two parts of this verse differently? Does 'all' mean 'all'?

A leper came to Jesus and besought Him, saying,

> 'Lord, if You are willing, You can make me clean.' Then Jesus put out His hand and touched him, saying, 'I am willing. Be cleansed'. And immediately his leprosy was cleansed. Matthew 8:2,3

The leper said, 'If you will, you can.' His dilemma, was one that faces so many believers today. He was saying in effect, 'I know that you can, but I don't know whether you are willing to.' The leper knew of Jesus' ability to make him clean but was uncertain of his will concerning healing. Jesus dispelled all doubt by saying 'I will'.

Many people have that same dilemma today. Yet, we have something that the leper did not have–the Word of God. His unbelief was excusable in a way that ours is not. For God has revealed His will in His Word. 'Jesus Christ is the same yesterday, today and forever' (Hebrews 13:8).

He has not changed. He is the same today. He is as willing to heal today as he was during His earthly ministry.

Some may reply, 'But doesn't the Bible say that suffering may come to believers?' This is true, but we need to see that although the English word 'suffer' may include the concept of sickness, in New Testament times it did not. Suffering and sickness were seen as very different from each other. Nowhere in the teaching or practice of Jesus did He promote sickness or tell anyone that it was inevitable or profitable. We must get back to the Bible!

Though the Bible teaches that the faithful believer may suffer persecution for his faith, suffering and sicknesses are not equated in the New Testament. Jesus clearly showed us that God is on the side of health.

Others speak of 'bearing their cross'. Yet on no occasion did Jesus even hint that our 'cross' involves sickness. Quite the opposite. He opposed sickness constantly throughout His ministry and taught His followers to do the same. He pointed out that their 'cross' might involve rejection, persecution, trials and for some even martyrdom for their faith, but never sickness.

God has even designed our bodies to be on the side of health. As soon as a germ enters our bodies, nature begins to repel it. When we break a bone or cut a finger, as long as our body is working properly, it does its utmost to repair and to heal and usually succeeds. Has God commanded our bodies to rebel against His will?

I recently spoke with a Christian medical doctor who had never really thought about these issues before. He had just accepted the teaching that sickness was from God, yet he had never considered how inconsistent such a view was with his profession.

In contrast, I shared how I could gladly be a doctor and go to the surgery daily with excitement, knowing that I was taking on the enemy in my fight against sickness and knowing that I was helping to take off people that which Satan had put on them. However I added that if I believed that sickness was sent by God, I could never be a doctor, for I would be fighting against God! If sickness is from God, then every doctor would be sinning in trying to take from people what God had put on them.

Not only is the teaching that God puts sickness on people unbiblical, but is also illogical. If God has put sickness on people then we have no right to do anything to remove it or alleviate it.

If sickness were the will of God, then every doctor would be a law-breaker and every nurse defying the Almighty. Every hospital would be a house of rebellion, instead of a place of mercy. If sickness were the will of God then instead of supporting hospitals we should be seeking to close them down! But I believe the Scriptures are clear–God is on the side of health.

I believe in doctors and nurses; I thank God for the medical profession; it is on the side of health, just as God is on the side of health. Yet some Christians are amazingly illogical. Declining prayer for healing, they say, 'It is God's will that I am sick.' Then the next day they go down to the doctors to get out of the will of God!

If you really believed that it was God's will that you were sick, you would never take any medicine or go to a doctor but, if we are honest, we don't really believe that. God is a good God.

The devil has propagated the idea that God puts sickness on people, because he knows that it will put the world off God, if they believe He is callous and uncaring. We have so swallowed this wrong concept of God that as I have already said, any disaster or anything bad that happens is called 'an act of God'.

Go back to the gospels and you will find a different Jesus to the one that is so often portrayed in many churches and Bible schools. You will find a Jesus who spent most of his time healing the sick. I meet Christians who have gone through three or four years of Bible school and yet have never heard about healing the sick. A respected theologian and Bible school tutor who recently heard me teach on this subject, came to me after the conference and said, 'You have turned my theology upside down. But what you are saying is biblical.' Could it be that we have invented a respectable 'evangelical Jesus', who is nothing like the real Jesus we read of in the Bible? Let's get back to the gospels and the Book of Acts. Pastors, let us read and preach our way through the gospels and fall in love afresh with the most loving and caring Saviour who still heals sick and suffering people today. Let us destroy the lies that the devil has spread about God. Let us go back to the Bible and reshape our thinking in line with the Word of God.

If I have still not convinced you that healing those who are sick is God's will, then notice how many Jesus healed during His earthly ministry.

> Now Jesus went about all Galilee, teaching in their synagogues, preaching the gospel of the Kingdom and healing all kinds of sickness and all kinds of disease among the people. Then His fame went throughout all Syria; and they brought to Him all sick people who were afflicted with various diseases and torments, and those who were demon-possessed, epileptics, and paralytics; and *He healed them.* Matthew 4:23,24

> When they had crossed over, they came to the land of Gennesaret and anchored there. And when they came out of the boat, immediately the people recognised Him, ran through the whole surrounding region, and began to carry about on beds those who were sick to wherever they heard He was. Wherever He entered into villages, cities, or the country, they laid the sick in the market-places, and begged Him that they might just touch the border of His garment. And *as many as touched Him were made well.* Mark 6:53–56

I cannot find one place in the Bible where Jesus ever refused to heal anyone who came in faith.

> And whole multitudes sought to touch Him, for power went out from Him and *healed them all.* Luke 6:19

> When evening had come they brought to Him many who were demon-possessed. And He cast out the spirits with a word and *healed all who were sick.* Matthew 8:16

Throughout the cities and villages He healed **every** sickness and **every** disease:

> Jesus went about all the cities and villages, teaching in their synagogues, preaching the gospel of the kingdom, and healing *every* sickness and *every* disease among the people. Matthew 9:35

> Great multitudes followed Him, and *He healed them all.* Matthew 12:15

> When Jesus went out He saw a great multitude; and He was moved with compassion for them and *healed their sick.* Matthew 14:14

He healed **all** the sick people who came to Him in Syria (Matthew 4:24). Again in Judea great multitudes followed Him and **He healed them** (Matthew 19:2):

> And Jesus departed from there, skirted the Sea of Galilee, and went up on the mountain and sat down

> there. Then great multitudes came to Him, having with them those who were lame, blind, mute, maimed, and many others; and they laid them down at Jesus' feet, and *He healed them*. So the multitude marvelled when they saw the mute speaking, the maimed made whole, the lame walking, and the blind seeing; and they glorified the God of Israel. Matthew 15:29–31

> Now when the sun was setting, all those who had anyone sick with various diseases brought them to Him; and He laid His hands on *every one of them and healed them*. Luke 4:40

> And the whole multitude sought to touch Him, for power went out from Him and *healed them all*. Luke 6:19

Jesus' attitude to sickness never varied. He healed all who came in faith. Has God changed or is He the very same God today that he was in Old and New Testament times?

In Malachi 3:6 we read, 'For I am the Lord, I do not change'. In Hebrews 13:8 we read, 'Jesus Christ is the same yesterday, and today and forever'. The Greek expression here for 'the same' is *ho autos* and means 'the very same identical person in every respect'.

Jesus' parting words were 'Lo, I am with you always, even unto the end of the age' (Matthew 28:20). He did not say 'I will be', which would have suggested a break. He said, 'I am', an unchanging presence, never withdrawn, a power to save and to heal as consistent as ever, even unto the end of the world.

Wherever in the Bible you find Jesus He was either on His way to heal someone or He was there healing someone or He had just left healing someone...and He is the same today!

When you read of the multitudes that came to Jesus and they were all healed, do you believe that had you been there, you would have been healed too? Well, if Jesus would have wanted to heal you then, you can be sure that He wants to heal you now. 'They were healed every one' would have included you, had you been sick and present there that day.

Healing, therefore, is for you today because God's will has never changed.

Jesus, who healed the sick and gave sight to the blind, still has compassion for those who suffer today. He who blessed the poor and forgave sinners then, is still the Saviour now. If people could come to Him and receive His mercy in Bible days, you or I can come to Him and receive His mercy today. If God's promises were good in Bible days, His promises are just as good today. If a leper could fall down before Him and receive healing then, a leper can fall down before Him and be miraculously cleansed today. If paralytics could rise and be whole at His command then, paralytics can be instantly healed through the power of His Word today.

From God's Word, I can come to no other conclusion than that it is God's perfect will to heal us all.

THOSE WHO ARE NOT YET HEALED

We know from past experience that not everyone we have prayed for has been healed so, we now have two options. Either we change the Word of God to fit into our experience, or we say, 'We are not where we should be in faith and experience. We are not where we want to be, but by God's grace, we are going to get there. We have a target. Lord, increase our faith; we too want to see everyone healed.'

Some believers brand Christians who believe these things so literally as 'fanatics' or 'extremists'. But what is a fanatic or an extremist? Is he someone who takes the Bible more literally than another or dares to take God at His Word?

I know that not everyone who is prayed for is healed, (we will consider this further in chapter seven) but we must never form our doctrines on the experiences of others or of our own.

I do not believe that it is God's will to heal the sick only when they are healed as I pray for them, but because the Bible says so. My faith is founded on God's Word and not on experience. I say these things not to condemn these who are at this time unhealed, but rather to lift their faith to keep believing, to help them stand in faith, believing that God wants them well!

Our faith relies on the two facts that God never changes and that His Word never changes.

Some Christians say 'But what about Joni?' or some other precious believer who has not been healed. But Joni is still alive. We cannot build a doctrine around other people's experience. While they are still alive, God can still heal them. I have seen many times God heal seemingly incurable people.

I am not writing this to condemn any who are not yet healed, but to encourage you that while you are still alive, there is always hope! Many Christians have been healed as they have continued to hold on in faith. Don't give up!

As these truths are preached, so, in the days ahead, I believe that we will see more and more the miracle power of God in our land.

Let us put our confidence afresh in the Word of God. In Matthew 21:22, Christ says, 'And all things, whatever you ask in prayer, believing, you will receive'. Does 'all things whatever you ask in prayer, believing,' include bodily sickness? YES!

> So Jesus answered and said to them, 'Have faith in God. For assuredly I say to you, whoever says to this mountain, "Be removed, and be cast into the sea" and does not doubt in his heart, but believes that those things he says will be done; he will have whatever he says. Therefore I say to you, whatever things you ask when you pray, believe that you receive them, and you will have them.' Mark 11:22–24

Does 'whatever things you desire, when ye pray' include bodily sickness? Then take Christ as your Healer. Jesus said:

> 'And whatever you ask in My Name, that I will do, that the Father may be glorified in the Son. If you ask anything in My Name, I will do it.' John 14:13,14

Does 'whatsoever ye shall ask in My Name' and 'if ye shall ask any thing in My Name' include bodily healing?

> 'And all things, whatever you ask in prayer, believing, you will receive.' Matthew 21:22

Does 'all things, whatever' include your sickness?

Some Christians are frightened of praying boldly lest they should pray against God's will, but He invites us to come boldly in prayer. Do not forget that it is our omniscient, omnipresent, almighty and sovereign God who has said, 'Whatever you ask in prayer, believing, you shall receive'.

> 'If you abide in Me, and My words abide in you, you will ask what you desire, and it shall be done for you.' John 15:7

Do these words 'You will ask what you desire and it will be done for you' include your sickness?

Rather than change the Word of God, we need to change our believing.

4 BY HIS STRIPES WE ARE HEALED

In this chapter (Isaiah 53), the expression 'to bear' occurs twice, but in relation to two different things. It is said not only that the Lord the righteous Servant bore our sins (v 12), but also that He bore our sicknesses (v 4). Thus His bearing our sicknesses as well as our sins forms an integral part of the Redeemer's work. Although He was without sin, He has borne our sins, and has done the same with our sicknesses.

As soon as a sick believer understands the meaning of the words, 'Jesus has borne my sins,' he is not afraid to say, 'I no longer need to bear my sins.' In the same way, as soon as He fully believes that Jesus has borne our sicknesses, he is not afraid to say, 'I no longer need to bear my sicknesses.' Jesus, in bearing sin, bore sickness also, which is its consequence. He has made payment for both, and He delivers us from both.

In Jesus, we have both pardon and healing; they are two sides of His redemptive work.

Andrew Murray, *Divine Healing*

The above was written in the late nineteenth century as a result of his being miraculously healed after two years out of the ministry due to sickness.

THE CROSS

I love the Old Testament, with the many revelations of the Christ who would come to save us. I love to read of God's dealings with men and women of faith. I also love the Epistles and the unfolding of such truths as justification and sanctification. I love to study the Book of Revelation too and to see an unfolding of God's plan. Most of all though, I love to read the gospels, for there we see when God became man and we see God's perfect will revealed. It is in the gospels that any doubts concerning God's goodness can be dispelled.

In chapter two we have seen how sickness, death and disease entered the world when man sinned. However, right back at the time when man first fell, God had a plan to restore to us all that Adam lost.

In Genesis chapter three, God revealed a glimpse of our Redeemer, who, though He would be wounded, would crush Satan's head, defeating him forever.

God warned the serpent that the seed of woman, 'shall bruise your head and you shalt bruise His heel' (Genesis 3:15). In the original Hebrew text two different words are used. The one born of woman would be 'bruised' or 'wounded', but the serpent's head would be 'crushed'. A bruised heel is painful. A crushed head is fatal.

The New International Version translates it correctly, 'And I will put enmity between you and the woman, and between your offspring and hers; he will crush your head, and you will strike his heel' Genesis 3:15 (NIV).

> For this purpose the Son of God was manifested, that He might destroy the works of the devil. 1 John 3:8

At the cross Jesus came to restore to us all that had been lost at the fall. The Bible tells us that 'Christ has redeemed us from the curse of the Law'. The curse of the Law was the penalty for breaking God's Law and included sickness, disease, emotional disturbances and poverty (Deuteronomy 28:27,28,35,60,61,65).

The prophet Isaiah foretold more than 700 years before Christ came to earth that He would bear not only our sins but that He would also bear our sicknesses and diseases.

> Surely He has borne our griefs [sicknesses or diseases], and carried our sorrows [pain] yet we esteemed Him stricken, smitten by God and afflicted. But He was wounded for our transgressions, He was bruised for our iniquities, the chastisement for our peace was upon Him; and with His stripes we are healed. Isaiah 53:4,5

Although the King James Version (KJV) translated the Hebrew words *kholee* as 'griefs' and *makob* as 'sorrows' the word *kholee* literally means 'sickness or affliction' and the word *makob* means 'pain'.

This is consistent with the KJV translation of *kholee* in other places like Deuteronomy 28:61, 1 Kings 17:17, 2 Kings 1:2; 8:8 and of *Makob* in places like Job 33:19 and Jeremiah 51:8.

Good Reference Bibles all have the marginal note by the words 'griefs' and 'sorrows' that the literal Hebrew words used by Isaiah are 'sicknesses' and 'diseases'. Young, the great Hebraist author of *Young's Concordance* translates it, 'Surely our sicknesses he hath borne and our pains he hath carried them' (Isaiah 53:4).

Dr Isaac Leeser's translation of the Hebrew Bible, as authorised for use by Orthodox Jews, reads:

> Our diseases did He bear Himself, and our pains He carried: while we indeed esteemed him smitten of God, and afflicted.

Matthew accurately quotes Isaiah in reference to Jesus' miracles: 'That it might be fulfilled which was spoken by Isaiah the prophet, saying, He Himself took our infirmities, and bore our sicknesses' (Matthew 8:17).

Isaiah 53 which speaks so clearly of the one who would be wounded for our transgressions and bruised for our iniquity, states that God dealt with our sicknesses and disease too in Christ's great substitutionary work on the cross. The correct translation of Isaiah 53:4 is: 'Surely [or certainly] he has borne our sicknesses, and carried our pains'. To prove that our sicknesses were carried away by Christ, just as our sins were carried away, the same Hebrew verb for 'borne' and 'carried' is used to describe both.

This verse, prefaced by the only 'surely' in the chapter, is the promise of healing. 'Surely', is the strongest statement of complete redemption from pain and sickness.

Satan has no right to lay on you what was laid on Jesus at the cross.

The Bible says that out of the mouth of two or three witnesses every word should be established (Matthew 18:16). Isaiah tells us 'Surely He has borne our sicknesses and our diseases...and by His stripes we are healed' (Isaiah 53:4,5). Matthew tells us 'that it might be fulfilled which was spoken by Isaiah the prophet, saying, "Himself took away our infirmities, and bare our sicknesses" ' (Matthew 8:17). Peter tells us 'who has Himself bore our sins in His own body on the tree that we, being dead to sin, should live unto righteousness: by His stripes you were healed' (1 Peter 2:24).

Isaiah, Matthew and Peter, three witnesses, all tell us that not only did Jesus shed His blood for the remission of our sins but that by His stripes we **were healed**!

The Bible then says that, 'With His stripes we are healed'. Notice that it does not say that we 'might be healed', that 'there is a possibility that we may be healed' nor even that 'we are going to be healed at some time in the future'. The Bible says 'we are healed'. God states it as a present tense fact rather than a future tense possibility.

Although Jesus paid for my sin nearly two thousand years ago, it is only as I believe that He died for me, that I enjoy God's forgiveness and the benefits of the cross. The same is true of healing. It is as I believe it, that I receive it.

Christians believe Isaiah 53:6 when it tells them that 'the Lord has laid on Him the iniquities of us all', so, why can we not therefore believe the whole of the passage, that 'He has borne our sicknesses and carried our pains?' The same passage that tells us that He bore our iniquities also tells us that our sicknesses and diseases were laid on Jesus too.

Just as I come to the cross and by faith see my sin laid on Jesus, then, by faith, I receive His forgiveness; so I now come to the cross and see my sickness laid on Jesus and by faith receive His divine health. At the cross Jesus defeated Satan, sickness and the power of sin. Therefore I can receive my healing by faith.

We receive healing as we see what Jesus accomplished nearly two thousand years ago for us. We see that we are healed by Christ's stripes, not that we are going to be healed or that there is a possibility that we could be healed. Just as with salvation, it is not until I realise what Christ accomplished for me on the cross that I can enjoy the full benefit of it and then receive the benefits by faith.

I cannot heal the sick. Jesus healed them nearly two thousand years ago. Others can receive their healing as they discover what is theirs in Christ and believe.

THE EARLY CHURCH

Like their Master, the early Church did not regard sickness as a friend to be welcomed, but as an enemy to be defeated.

Jesus gave his disciples the command to heal the sick:

> And when He had called His twelve disciples to Him, He gave them power over unclean spirits, to cast them out, and to heal all kinds of sickness and all kinds of disease. Matthew 10:1

Jesus never commissioned anyone to preach the gospel without including healing for the sick. He said, 'Into whatever city you enter... heal the sick that are there'. That command applies to those in ministry today. This commission was not limited to the first apostles. Jesus said of all believers:

> 'These signs will follow those who believe: in My Name they will cast out demons; they will speak with new tongues... they will lay hands on the sick, and they will recover.' Mark 16:17,18

If we believe they will, they will. If we do not believe, they will not.

Christ's promise for the spirit, that it shall be saved, is in the great commission and is for all. His promise for the body, that it shall recover, is also in His commission. To deny that one part of Christ's commission is for us today, is to deny that the other part is for us today.

He said of believers:

> 'Most assuredly, I say to you, he who believes in Me, the works that I do he will do also, and greater works than these he will do, because I go to My Father. And whatever you ask in My Name, that I will do, that the Father may be glorified in the Son. If you ask anything in My Name, I will do it.' John 14:12–14

He did not say these 'greater works' will follow apostles, pastors, and spiritual giants, but 'he who believes in Me'.

After His ascension, Jesus poured out the Holy Spirit on the Church to continue what He had begun. Listen to how the early Church prayed!

> 'Now, Lord, look on their threats, and grant to Your servants, that with all boldness they may speak Your word, by stretching out Your hand to heal and that signs and wonders may be done through the Name of Your holy servant Jesus.' Acts 4:29,30

Just as with Jesus, the early Church expected miracles:

> And the multitudes with one accord heeded the things spoken by Philip, hearing and seeing the miracles which he did. For unclean spirits, crying with a loud voice, came out of many, who were possessed; and many who were paralysed and lame were healed. Acts 8:6,7

As a result, many turned to the Lord. When Aeneas, who had been bedridden for eight years, was healed 'all who lived at Lydda and Sharon saw him and turned to the Lord' (Acts 9:35).

Notice what happened shortly after Christ was raised from the dead, (an example of God's will wherever the gospel is preached):

> And through the hands of the apostles many signs and wonders were done among the people...and believers were increasingly added to the Lord, multitudes of both men and women, so that they brought the sick out into the streets, and laid them on beds and couches, that at least the shadow of Peter passing by might fall on some of them. Also a multitude gathered from the surrounding cities to Jerusalem, bringing sick people and those who were tormented by unclean spirits; and *they were all healed.* Acts 5:12–16

God's purpose and will had not changed after Christ's ascension.

James wrote to the early believers:

> Is anyone among you sick? Let him call for the elders of the church, and let them pray over him, anointing him with oil in the Name of the Lord; and the prayer of faith will save the sick and the Lord will raise him up. James 5:14,15

This passage implies that sickness was not a common occurrence in the early church. James asks the question 'Is any sick among you?' He does not assume that there were. He does not refer to the elders praying and anointing 'all the sick in the Church'. Would he write to our churches today 'Is any sick among you?'

Around the fourth century AD a concept that is still around today crept into the Church, that the body was unimportant and that only the spirit is important. This led to a despising of the body, rather than a New Testament emphasis on Christ's healing power. Last rites replaced anointing the body for healing. Yet this negative view of the body is not what the Bible teaches. Our bodies are important. They are in fact the temple of the Holy Spirit! (1 Corinthians 3:16,17; 6:19).

We are the 'Body of Christ' (1 Corinthians 12:27, Ephesians 5:30). How can it be the will of God for the Body of Christ to be sick?

It is interesting that the religious leaders often criticised Jesus for healing on the Sabbath. Yet this reaction resembles the idea of healing held by many today. They consider the body as 'secular' and of little importance to God.

Isn't it interesting how the Lord deliberately and purposely healed on the Sabbath day, exposing this godless idea and demonstrating that the body's restoration was a part of God's plan?

> 'Beloved, I wish above all things that thou mayest prosper and be in health, even as thy soul prospers.' 3 John 2

God's best is that we live in health. It might be worth mentioning that we should use our faith to live healthily and not just to get healed! Read these words again:

> 'Beloved, I wish above all things that thou mayest prosper and be in health, even as thy soul prospers.'

Isn't it amazing that, after many years as a believer, John's greatest desire and wish for the believers was that they might be as physically well as they were spiritually well. His prayerful desire was that they should be as physically well (in health) as they were spiritually well (as their soul prospered). After three years of being with Jesus and many years of faithfully serving the Lord this was the thing that he desired above all else.

Yet it is even more exciting to read these words, realising that they are not just the desires of a man, but inspired by God. This is God's desire! If we believe the Bible to be the inspired Word of God, then these words expressed by John are not just John's sentiments but from the heart of God, who says to the believer, 'I wish above all things that thou mayest prosper and be in health even as thy soul prospers'. Surely this puts an end to all doubt about God's will concerning healing.

God is on the side of health!

Let us summarise some of the truths that we have seen together.

God's Word is not confusing about healing–for Jesus is the Word of God made flesh (John 1:14)

God never changes: His attitude to sickness and disease is the same as it was when Jesus walked this earth

'They were healed –everyone' was experienced by the entire nation of Israel: 'There was not one feeble person among their tribes'

The same was experienced by everyone in the throngs which followed Jesus: 'Great multitudes followed Him, and He healed them all'

'As many (sinners) as received Him, to them He gave the right to become the children of God' (John 1:12). As many (sick) as touched Him were made perfectly whole (Matthew 14:36, Mark 6:56)

God's Word is His will: when we read what He promises to do, we know what it is His will to do

Jesus came to show us what God's will is concerning healing and He is the same today

Don't let any obstacle of unbelief get in the way of receiving your healing.

A woman with a haemorrhage came to Jesus (Luke 8:43–48). Despite her years of receiving medication the doctors had been unable to help; in fact she was getting worse. When she reached Jesus the situation looked hopeless. He was surrounded by a crowd. In fact, it seemed that everything was there to stop her from receiving healing. But she said, 'If I may touch but the hem of His garment I shall be made whole.' I assume that she got down on her knees and crawled through the legs of the crowd, (otherwise she must have been very short to touch the hem of His garment!). Nothing was going to stop her getting to Jesus. Like this lady, we must not give up! Like her, you might not be able to touch Jesus physically, but you can touch Him by faith.

The healing of this woman shows us that our own faith can initiate healing. You don't have to wait for God to move on your behalf. This woman had spent all her money on physicians but had just grown worse. Still she said, 'If I may touch but His garments I shall be made whole.' Immediately 'the fountain of her blood was dried up'.

It was not Jesus' garment that healed her. Jesus told her, 'Daughter, your faith has made you well' (Mark 5:34).

Some men had a similar problem in trying to bring their friend to Jesus. They could not get near to the house that He was in because of the vast crowd. No doubt the devil told them, 'It is obviously not God's will for your friend to be healed'. Yet they would not give up. They 'raised the roof for a miracle' (Mark 2:1–12).

Use your faith to raise the roof for a miracle! Don't let anything stop you. Don't listen to the doubts of the enemy.

RECEIVE THE SAVIOUR

If you have never received the Lord Jesus Christ as your personal Saviour, the greatest need in your life is to know God's forgiveness. We have all sinned and failed to meet God's righteous requirements, but because Jesus died on the Cross as our substitute we can know God's forgiveness.

The Bible tells us that sin separates us from God. 'Your iniquities have separated you from your God: and your sins have hidden His face from you, so that He will not hear' (Isaiah 59:2). Sin separates us from friendship with God in this life and ultimately will separate us from God for eternity, unless we receive His forgiveness.

Over the years I have had the joy of seeing thousands of people miraculously healed of all manner of disease and physical disabilities. However, always before I pray for the healing of their sick bodies, I like to give them the opportunity to receive the assurance of God's forgiveness.

Jesus said to a paralytic who was brought to Him for healing, 'Your sins are forgiven you'; then he added, 'Arise, take up your bed and go your way into your house'. Forgiveness came first, and then healing (Mark 2:5,11). Before the

Lord healed He said to him 'your sins are forgiven you'. Forgiveness came first.

Healing is important, but our greatest need is for God's forgiveness. Jesus died in our place. On the cross He bore the punishment for our sin, that we might be forgiven. Forgiveness is now freely available to you and to me.

> If we confess our sins, He is faithful and just to forgive us our sins and to cleanse us from all unrighteousness.
> 1 John 1:9

If you will own up to your sin and ask God to forgive you, He will. 'The free gift of God is eternal life through Jesus Christ our Lord' (Romans 6:23).

The greatest miracle that ever happens is when someone gives his or her life to Christ. Jesus can heal you, but first things first. Receive the forgiveness of God. Pray this prayer now:

> *'Dear Lord Jesus, I thank you that you died for me. Thank you that you bore my sins on the cross, so that I could be forgiven. I am so grateful. Now I give my life to you. I turn from my sin and ask for Your forgiveness. I want to live for You, Lord Jesus. Come into my life as my Saviour and Lord. Thank you Jesus, that you hear my prayer and You save me right now. In Your precious Name. Amen.'*

If you have prayed this prayer and truly meant it, the Lord Jesus has come into your life and God has forgiven your sins. Now seek to talk with Jesus daily in prayer, to study His Word, the Bible everyday, that your faith may grow and to tell others that you have prayed this prayer and received Jesus Christ.

Now I want to pray for your healing. 'Jesus Christ is the same yesterday, today and forever' (Hebrews 13:8). The same Jesus who walked the shores of Galilee, who healed the sick, cleansed the lepers and relieved the oppressed is here right now. His power is the same as it was then. His promises have never changed and His power has never changed. He is as merciful and compassionate as He ever was.

Jesus said, 'If two of you agree on earth concerning anything that you ask, it will be done for them by My Father in heaven' (Matthew 18:19). There is power in the prayer of agreement. Let us agree together for the Lord to touch you and make you whole:

'Heavenly Father, I come to You in the Name of Jesus, who bore all my sins and sicknesses. Your Word says that by His stripes I am healed. So now, in faith, I receive my healing. I confess every sin, wrong attitude, fear and resentment. Forgive me as I forgive others now. I believe that this sickness and infirmity must go in Jesus' Name and by Your mighty power. I break its hold over my life and I am set free, in Jesus' Name. Thank you that you said; "Whatever we ask in faith believing we shall receive". I believe your Word and I receive my healing now by faith, in Jesus' Name. Amen.'

5 NOW WHAT DO I DO?

While I was at camp, the Lord healed me of arthritis in my feet.

I just knew deep down inside that God had healed me but, when I walked away to my caravan the pain was still awful. But, as I was walking and telling the Lord about it, something inside said, 'So what'. God had healed me and I knew it!

My problem now was how to tell people that God had healed me when I was walking like a cripple. I believed God, but I didn't think that others would. Yet I knew inside that I was healed.

This continued for a fortnight. Then I heard someone say, 'When you have got God's 'yes' on the inside, ignore the enemy's 'no' on the outside.' *I claimed that word and have been free from pain ever since.*

Oh, the joy of being able to stand in a meeting singing and praising God. To be able to sleep at night instead of living in agony everytime I go to bed and to be able to stand and do jobs without pain. Thank you Jesus. He is so wonderful, but I know that this is only a foretaste of what God has for me and all who will love and obey Him.

Bless you Peter, keep up the good work and may the Lord continue to bless and use you.

Betty.

One of the many lovely letters we receive at our offices each week from those who receive their healing as they stand on the promises of God. (Used with permission.)

After you have received prayer, let me share with you three important keys to receiving your healing.

1. RECEIVE BY FAITH

First, I must receive the answer to my prayer by faith.

The world says, 'When I see it, I'll believe it'. God says 'When you believe it, you will see it'.

Notice which comes first–believing or receiving?

Jesus said:

> 'Therefore I say to you, whatever things you ask when you pray, believe that you receive them, and you will have them.' Mark 11:24

Jesus first promised all that we need, 'Whatever you ask, when you pray [not after you get well, but while you are still sick–'when you pray'], believe that you receive them, and you shall have them'. Notice the order: 'When you pray, believe that you receive'.

Most people have this reversed. They think it should be this way: 'Whatever you desire, pray for it, and when you see and feel it, then believe that you have received it'.

However, there must come a moment when we stop asking God to heal us and receive our healing by faith. We stand on the promises of God's Word. As a result, we receive an inner confidence that our prayers have been answered.

To pray with faith does not mean to beg and to plead for healing. Remember, if you have accepted Christ as your personal Saviour, then you are a child of God, and He is your Father. You are not a beggar. The Father wants you to come to Him as any child comes to loving parents. Come with confidence.

> Faith means we are confident of what we hope for, convinced of what we do not see. Hebrews 11:1 (Moffatt Translation)

Our faith in God's Word provides the confidence that we

are healed. The fact that God has said it is enough. Real faith rests entirely on what the Word of God says.

In this life there is a continual battle between our senses and our faith. Our senses war and revolt against God's Word. They argue and fight, saying, 'That is not so, because it cannot yet be felt and seen.' But faith calmly declares: 'It is written. God's Word declares it, so it is true.'

To walk by faith means to give God's Word the pre-eminence over our senses. To walk by sight means to give our senses the pre-eminence over God's Word.

Many Christians say, 'If I could see a change, I would believe'. But that is not believing, that is seeing. They say, 'If I could just feel better, I would believe'. That is not believing, that is feeling. You do not believe with your eyes, you see with them. You do not believe with your ears, you hear with them. You do not believe with your feelings, you feel with them. You believe with your heart; it is an internal thing.

People often say, 'I will believe, when I feel better'. But that is not faith. It is easy to believe when the pain is gone! Faith always has to operate before you see any evidence. Faith is believing despite any physical evidence. I believe I am going to heaven before I get there. I have never seen heaven, or felt it, but I believe it is a reality. Faith will hold on to God's promises, even when there is no immediate evidence.

Faith does not pretend that there is no problem or pain, but is confident in God's faithfulness to His Word and that a miracle is on the way.

Faith rests in the promises of God. Jesus compared the Kingdom of God to a man who sowed a seed and went home to sleep. Once the seed has been sown he does not dig it up to inspect it, if he did he would kill the seed. He simply rests, knowing that the work has begun.

When Peter took a step of faith and got out of the boat to walk on water, the first thing that robbed him of the miracle was the things he **felt**. He felt the wind blow around him. The second thing was he **saw** the threatening waves. What he felt and saw shook his faith and caused him to take his eyes off Jesus. Our faith needs to be in God's Word, not in what we see or feel.

Jesus rebuked a fig tree which bore no figs. He spoke to the tree, 'No one shall eat fruit of you hereafter for ever'. The moment He spoke, He knew that the life of the tree died and that the tree would soon wither.

The following day He passed by the tree again with His disciples and 'saw the fig tree dried up from the roots'. Peter suddenly remembered what the Lord had said to the tree the day before and exclaimed in amazement: 'Master, behold, the fig tree which you cursed is withered away' (Mark 11:21–24 AV).

Jesus replied, 'Have faith in God'. He had expected the tree to wither and what He had believed for had happened. We must not doubt because we do not see the green leaves (or symptoms) wither immediately.

When I speak the words, 'In Jesus Name be made whole. Sickness leave!' I see by faith the axe laid to the root of the problem and believe that the symptoms will wither and go. I get my information from God's Word instead of from my body. My body then has to catch up with my faith.

2. BEGIN TO DO WHAT YOU COULD NOT DO BEFORE

In most of our crusades around the world there are too many people in the meetings to lay hands on each one individually. So I usually encourage people to lay hands on themselves, as I pray. Then I tell them to begin to do what they could not do before. It is interesting to note how many are healed as they simply take such a step of faith.

In Acts chapter 3 we read of the lame beggar at the Temple Gate:

> Then Peter said, 'Silver and gold do I not have, but what I do have I give to you. In the Name of Jesus Christ of

> Nazareth rise up and walk' and he took him by the right hand and lifted him up, and immediately his feet and ankle bones received strength. Acts 3:6,7

Notice that the scriptures do not say his feet and ankles were strengthened and then Peter lifted him. It says as he lifted him, 'immediately his feet and ankle bones received strength'. It was as the man took a step of faith that he received his miracle.

The man could have answered Peter's command to 'Rise up and walk', with the words, 'I can't, I am lame'. But as he took a step of faith and stood, at that moment he was healed.

In the same way, I encourage people to begin to do what they could not do before. If they could not see, I tell them to close their eyes as I pray and then to open them and to begin to focus. If their friend has been deaf, I tell them to whisper in their friend's ear. If they could not walk, I tell them to begin to stand in Jesus' Name, to take a step of faith. If they could not speak before, I tell them to begin to form words and to speak them out in Jesus' Name. If they had arthritic knees, I tell them to start walking and bending their knees.

Soon there is a queue of people wanting to testify to receiving their healing. One night recently around 1,000 people queued to testify to receiving a healing miracle in just that one meeting!

As people hear the testimonies, their faith rises and many more are healed.

Secular newspapers have carried reports of the miracles in our crusades around the world. One Muslim newspaper recently carried the front page story 'Miracles'. The Muslim reporter said, 'I've seen it with my own eyes! The blind see, the deaf hear and the lame walk.' The paper carried photographs and stories of twenty of the people the man had interviewed, including a girl who had been insane for fourteen years and had been brought thirty miles in an ox-drawn cart by her parents. She was now healed and in her right mind.

As they take a step of faith I have seen so many receive their healing as they begin to do what they could not do before.

On one occasion, during a large tent crusade, I prayed for a woman who could hardly move because of arthritis. I felt the Lord's prompting me to tell her to walk around the tent and by faith to walk into her new health. She set off with her friend and I continued to pray with others that had come for prayer. A few minutes later, the woman returned testifying that as she began to walk by faith, the Lord touched her and completely healed her. She had run the rest of the way around the tent to quickly tell me what had happened.

When four men came carrying their friend who was paralysed and let him down through the roof, Jesus, 'seeing their faith' (not hearing them talk about how much faith they had), healed him. He saw faith in their actions (Mark 2:1–12).

Jesus told the paralytic to rise, take up his bed and to go his way. The man did not focus on his paralysis; he did what Jesus told him.

Action is the proof of what we believe.

It is commonly assumed that the paralytic was healed through the faith of his friends. However, this is not completely true. He had to take his own step of faith, he was not healed prostrate on his mat. He had to rise up and walk. He had to stand on the words of Jesus.

Jesus told the man with the withered hand to stretch forth his hand. As the man took that step of faith, his hand was restored (Mark 3:1–5).

It is interesting how often Jesus encouraged people to do something, to take a step of faith. As they responded to His voice, they received. Peter had to get out of the boat to walk on the water. Jesus didn't send the water into the boat to get him out. He had to respond to Jesus and take a step in obedience (Matthew 14:22–32).

Like Peter, when we focus on our circumstances we will sink; but we must look to Jesus for He is the master of the winds and waves.

Jesus told the blind man to 'Go and wash in the pool of Siloam'. He encouraged the man to put actions behind his faith. The man was not healed until he acted in faith (John 9:7). In the same way the Lord sent the ten lepers to show themselves to the priest. None of them were healed when they left Jesus, it was only as they went that they were cleansed (Luke 17:14).

At Peter's house his mother-in-law was in bed, sick with a fever. Jesus rebuked the fever. Then 'He took her by the hand, and lifted her up, and immediately the fever left her' (Mark 1:29–31). This is a perfect example of faith in action:

(1) He rebuked the fever
(2) He made her arise in faith
(3) the fever left her.

3. HOLD ON

The Bible tells us that it is 'by faith and patience' that we inherit the promises (Hebrews 6:12).

Faith takes hold of God's promises and patience keeps hold until we receive the answer.

For twenty-five years Abraham held on to God's promise of a child! Many of us would have given up after twenty-five weeks! Abraham held on until he had received what God had promised. Sometimes we have to hold on in faith too. God said it; that settles it!

Paul says of Abraham: 'Not being weak in faith, he did not consider his own body, already dead (since he was about a hundred years old), and the deadness of Sarah's womb. He did not waver at the promise of God through unbelief, but was strengthened in faith, giving glory to God, and being fully convinced that what He had promised He was also able to perform' (Romans 4:19–21). Abraham chose not to believe these circumstances; he chose to believe God!

Sometimes we instantly see the result of our praying, sometimes we do not.

It seems that the Lord heals in three main ways:

An Instantaneous Miracle

'And immediately he received his sight' (Mark 10:52). This is what we should believe for.

There is Some Improvement, but not Complete Healing

Jesus said to a blind man, 'Do you see?' and he replied, 'I see men, but they are like trees walking'. (Mark 8:24). This account gives us great encouragement; since Jesus needed to minister to this man twice. The first time the man could see better than before, but his sight was still blurred, so Jesus ministered to him a second time and he was totally healed.

If you have been prayed for and are not completely healed yet, don't give up–hold on! As we await our healing we need to ensure that there is no sin which could hinder it (Exodus 15:26). **Unconfessed sin** (1 Corinthians 11:29,30) or **past occult involvement** are common blockages. Some people even have a reluctance to being completely healed (John 5:1–8; Mark 10:51). **Resentment** can also prevent us from receiving our healing (Mark 11:26). If there is anyone we resent, we must forgive them. **Spiritual unrest**, **emotional trauma** and **damaged relationships** lie behind many illnesses. This should not surprise us as the Bible mentions the relationship between our body, mind and spirit (Psalm 38:3, Proverbs 3:2–8, 14–30). What goes on in one affects the others. Sometimes a delay in receiving healing has a root cause. Allow the Lord to speak to your heart and show you if there are any blockages.

Some people ask the question, 'As I have been prayed for before, can I be prayed for again?' I would say that if you have new faith to receive your miracle, then the answer is 'Yes!' However, sometimes it is right to just hold on, and to keep believing for a completion of your miracle.

No Immediate Evidence of Healing

This is when we really need to stand in faith. I have heard Christians say, 'In Bible days people were always healed instantly'. However, this is not true. The nobleman's son 'began to amend' from the hour that Jesus ministered to him (John 4:52 AV). He began to get better from that hour.

Jesus said to believers, 'They shall lay hands on the sick and they shall recover' (Mark 16:18). Some are healed instantly, others 'recover'. They receive their healing by faith, believing that a miracle has begun and continue to hold on until they are completely whole.

Jesus sent the lepers to the priest to certify that they had been healed. Yet, when they started on their journey, they were as sick as they had ever been. They were healed 'as they went' (Luke 17:14).

The implication of the passages is that they walked into their healing, step by step. They came to Jesus: Point A. He sent them to the priest: Point B. Between Point A and Point B they were healed. All the journey they walked by faith.

Though at the time there was no evidence to prove their healing, they stood on Jesus' words and received what they had believed for.

Even if there is no immediate evidence of healing after prayer, do not lose heart. Do not give up and say, 'It is obviously not God's will'. Hold on to His promises.

1. Receive by faith
2. Begin to do what you could not do before
3. Hold on!

6 What was Paul's thorn in the flesh?

'I heard a great number of people testify that they had been healed by simply trusting the Word of Christ, just as they would for their salvation. It drove me to my Bible. I determined that I must settle this matter one way or another. I am so glad I did not go to a man. At His feet, alone, with my Bible open, and with no one to help or guide me, I became convinced that this was part of Christ's glorious gospel for a sinful and suffering world, and the purchase of His precious cross, for all who would believe and receive His Word.'

A.W. Simpson, Founder of the
Evangelical and Missionary Alliance
Gospel of healing (Used with permission.)

You would be amazed at the different interpretations that I have heard concerning the passage where Paul refers to his 'thorn in the flesh'. I have heard it preached that Paul's thorn was everything from a hunch-back and malaria, to an eye problem and an unconverted mother-in-law!

Such bizarre interpretations arise from a lack of knowledge of the biblical metaphor, 'a thorn in the flesh' or 'a thorn in the side'.

The term was not unique to Paul. In fact, as a man saturated in the Old Testament writings, it was a term he would have been very familiar with.

In Numbers 33:55, Moses uses the term to refer to those who were harassing God's people. Joshua also described

Israel's enemies as a 'thorn' (Joshua 23:13). In Judges 2:3, the Lord warned Israel that He would drive their enemies out, but that they would be 'thorns in their side', because of Israel's disobedience.

It is worth noting that in Scripture the term is used of those who create difficulties for, and oppose God's people. It was always used in the context of people and never about such things as sickness.

Is Paul therefore referring to people as his 'thorn in the flesh'?

I believe that if we read the passage in context we will see that this is so. So often these verses are quoted out of context and as such could be used to promote any bizarre theory. However, if we read the preceding verses, the context becomes clear, that he is referring to those who opposed him and rejected his message. As I am sure that you are aware, Paul did not write his letter to the Corinthian Church in chapters. These were added many centuries later. The confusion surrounding this passage comes when we read chapter 12 of 2 Corinthians and fail to see that it flows straight on from chapter 11.

Let us look at the passage in context:

Chapter 11

24 From the Jews five times I received forty stripes minus one.
25 Three times I was beaten with rods; once I was stoned; three times I was shipwrecked; a night and a day I have been in the deep;
26 in journeys often, in perils of waters, in perils of robbers, in perils of my own countrymen, in perils of the Gentiles, in perils in the city, in perils in the wilderness, in perils in the sea, in perils among false brethren;
27 in weariness and toil, in sleeplessness often, in hunger and thirst, in fastings often, in cold and nakedness–
28 besides the other things, what comes upon me daily: my deep concern for all the churches.
29 Who is weak, and I am not weak? Who is made to stumble, and I do not burn with indignation?
30 If I must boast, I will boast in the things which concern my infirmity.

31 The God and Father of our Lord Jesus Christ, who is blessed forever, knows that I am not lying,
32 In Damascus the governor, under Aretas the king, was guarding the city of the Damascenes with a garrison, desiring to apprehend me;
33 but I was let down in a basket through a window in the wall, and escaped from his hands.

Chapter 12
It is doubtless not profitable for me to boast. I will come to visions and revelations of the Lord.
2 I know a man in Christ who fourteen years ago whether in the body I do not know, or whether out of the body I do not know, God knows–such a one was caught up to the third heaven.
3 And I know such a man–whether in the body or out of the body I do not know, God knows–
4 how he was caught up into Paradise and heard inexpressible words, which it is not lawful for a man to utter.
5 Of such a one I will boast; yet of myself I will not boast, except in my infirmities.
6 For though I might desire to boast, I will not be a fool; for I will speak the truth. But I forbear, lest anyone should think of me above what he sees me to be or hears from me.
7 And *lest I should be exalted above measure by the abundance of the revelations, a thorn in the flesh was given to me, a messenger of Satan to buffet me, lest I should be exalted above measure.*
8 Concerning this thing I pleaded with the Lord three times that it might depart from me.
9 And He said to me, 'My grace is sufficient for you, for My strength is made perfect in weakness.' Therefore most gladly I will rather boast in my infirmities that the power of Christ may rest upon me.
10 Therefore I take pleasure in infirmities, in reproaches, in needs, in persecutions, in distresses, for Christ's sake. For when I am weak, then I am strong.

No wonder Paul was weak, beaten, shipwrecked, without food and on one occasion even left for dead! No wonder he prayed that God would take this thorn away!

The opposition Paul received was a part of keeping him humble. Not only had Paul been mightily used by the Lord in reaching the lost and in church planting, but he had also received some powerful visions and revelations (12:1) and even been caught up into paradise.

'And lest I should be exalted above measure by the abundance of revelations a thorn in the flesh was given to me, a messenger of Satan to buffet me, lest I be exalted above measure' (1 Corinthians 12:7). If you think that you have a 'thorn in the flesh', it is worth asking where your abundance of revelation is.

What is more, not only do we have the Old Testament use of the word, the context of Paul's writings and the purpose of his 'thorn' given, but notice the source of his 'thorn in the flesh'–Satan.

This was no blessing from heaven, but from the enemy.

One Bible commentator referred to Paul's thorn as partial blindness caused by the brightness of Divine light as the Lord appeared to him at his conversion. Yet would it not be blasphemy to refer to partial blindness caused by a glimpse of the glorified Christ as 'a messenger of Satan?' (1 Corinthians 12:7)

Paul calls this thorn 'a messenger (*angelos* in the Greek) of Satan', literally the angel of the devil, or Satan's angel. It is interesting that of the 188 times the Greek word *angelos* appears in the Bible, it is translated 'angel' 181 times and 'messenger' the other 7 times. On every occasion it is a reference to a person and not to an inanimate thing.

Notice too that this 'messenger of Satan' was sent to buffet Paul. The word 'buffet' means blow after blow, as when waves buffet a boat. This is no static disease like opthalmia but a recurrent beating, blow after blow.

One only has to read the Book of Acts to see that from the moment of his conversion, the Jews tried to take his life (9:2,23,29).

He was persecuted and expelled at Antioch (13:44–50), and mobbed and nearly stoned at Iconium. (14:1–5). He fled to Lystra where, despite the wonderful healing of the man who had been crippled, he was stoned by the multitudes and left for dead (14:16–19). He rose up and continued, only to be whipped, beaten and jailed at Philippi (16:16–40), mobbed and made to escape from Thessalonica (17:1–10), mobbed and made to flee from Berea (17:10–14), opposed at Corinth (18:1–17), and the cause of a riot at Ephesus (19:23–31). From start to finish there were constant plots being made by the Jews to take his life (20:3).

> 'From the Jews five times I received forty stripes minus one. Three times I was beaten with rods; once I was stoned; three times I was shipwrecked; a night and a day I have been in the deep; in journeys often, in perils of waters, in perils of robbers, in perils of my own countrymen, in perils of the Gentiles, in perils in the city, in perils in the wilderness, in perils in the sea, in perils among false brethren; in weariness and toil, in sleeplessness often, in hunger and thirst, in fastings often, in cold and nakedness–besides the other things, what comes upon me daily: my deep concern for all the churches.' 2 Corinthians 2:24–28

Notice that Paul mentions just about everything **except** sickness. Why substitute sickness, as an explanation of his thorn in the flesh, when he does not mention sickness among all of these buffetings?

Paul had once persecuted the Christians and now he was beginning to experience the same and greater persecution.

Nowhere does Paul imply that his 'thorn in the flesh' was a sickness or disease. Yet it has been one of the most prevalent objections to the ministry of healing.

Some have quoted Galatians 6:11 to suggest that Paul had defective eyesight. 'You see how large a letter I have written unto you with mine own hand' (Galatians 6:11). But the word 'letter' used here is translated from the same Greek word as in 2 Corinthians 3:6 and does not refer to a letter of the alphabet. The word 'large' used here means the quantative kind and is a reference to the length of his epistle. It is inconsistant to suggest that Paul had defective eyesight when we read in Acts 9:18 that God healed him.

In closing let me say that even if Paul's thorn had been a

physical disorder, it did not hinder the faith of the people in Ephesus (Acts 19:11,12), Melita (Acts 28:8,9) and Lystra (Acts 14:8). They received healing, so do not let any interpretation of this passage hinder your faith to receive healing either!

It is amazing how eagerly some Christians will set aside all the positive teachings on healing in Scripture and misquote this 'thorn in the flesh' passage to discount it! The weight of Scripture is quite overwhelming, showing that God is both able and willing to heal today.

Some like to point out that Timothy had stomach problems (1 Timothy 5:23). Trophimus had to remain at Miletus (2 Timothy 4:20) and Epaphroditus was taken ill (Philippians 2:27).

These verses present no problem to those who believe in God's power and willingness to heal the sick today. We are all more than aware that the enemy will try to rob us of our health. However, look at Paul's advice to Timothy: 'Take a little wine for your stomach's sake.' His advice was that the young man should take measures to improve his health. Paul was encouraging the young man to do all that he could to get better. He did not advise him to passively accept his sickness, as some do today. Paul obviously believed that it was God's will to restore Timothy to health, as he would not have encouraged his friend to get out of God's will. The problem we have today is that Christians say, 'It is God's will that I am sick,' and then the next day they go down to the doctor to get out of the will of God!

Epaphroditus was also ill and Paul gives us the reason why: 'For the work of Christ he was near unto death, not regarding his life.' Epaphroditus had been overdoing it. So Paul had to leave him behind to recover. There is a warning here that our health may suffer if we do not regard God's guidelines for rest and take care of our bodies.

As we close this chapter, let me say that if any of the teaching on Paul's thorn in the flesh being sickness has hindered your believing for a miracle in the past, it would be good to now re-read chapters one to five of this book, that your faith might rise to receive your healing from Jesus.

7 Forty Common Questions Concerning Healing

My son, give attention to My Words;
incline your ear to My sayings.
Do not let them depart from your eyes;
keep them in the midst of your heart;
for they are life to those who find them,
and health to all their flesh.

Proverbs 4:20–22

Question 1 — *Doesn't God send sickness on people?*

Some people quote Exodus 15:26: 'If you diligently heed the voice of the Lord your God and do what is right in His sight and give ear to His commandments and keep all His statutes, I will put none of the diseases upon you which I have brought upon the Egyptians. For I am the Lord who heals you.'

In a similar way, some versions translate Isaiah 45:7, 'I form the light and create darkness, I make peace and create evil. I, the Lord, do all these things'.

Yet we know that God does not create evil. Evil does not proceed from God. Though He permits evil, He does not initiate it. Nor does He cause sickness. Dr Robert Young, the author of *Young's Analytical Concordance to the Bible*, an outstanding Hebrew and Greek scholar, states in his book, *Hints and Helps to Biblical Interpretation* that in Exodus 15:26 the literal Hebrew reads 'I will permit to be put upon thee none of the diseases which I have permitted to be brought upon the Egyptians, for I am the Lord that healeth thee.'

It is here that we see the mis-translation in some versions of the Bible. The active verb in the Hebrew has been translated in the causative sense whereas it should have been translated in the permissive sense. We must not be confused between permission and commission. God permits people to steal and kill but He certainly does not commission it. There is a vast difference between what God allows and what God actively causes. God does not cause sickness.

QUESTION **2**

Is sickness redemptive? I heard it preached that when we suffer pain and illness we are joined to Christ in His suffering for the salvation of the world. Is this true?

No, it is not. Jesus' death on the cross was all-sufficient for our salvation. Our own suffering cannot add to the wonderful work of Calvary, neither does it need any adding to.

It is also worth noting that when Jesus talks about suffering for the Gospel's sake, He was not talking about sickness and disease, but concerning the persecution that may come to those who live godly lives. Jesus never encouraged anyone to just accept their sickness as a gift from God. Whenever He encountered illness and disease he regarded them as enemies from which people should be set free.

QUESTION **3**

When I asked my minister to anoint me with oil and pray for my healing according to James 5:14,15, he told me that the book of James was written to the Jews and not to the Church. Is this true?

I have heard this objection to this passage before. One preacher even suggested that the Epistle is written for the Jews of the tribulation period. He declared that the word translated 'Church' in James 5:14 should read 'synagogue', yet this is not so.

The word used is *ekklésia*, Church, not *sunagógé* for synagogue. The word *ekklésia* comes from *ek* 'out of' and *kaleo* 'to call'. It is 'those called to Christ out of the world', a term used in the Bible for 'believers'.

James also addresses the epistle to 'my beloved *(agapétoi)* brethren', (James 1:16,19; 2:5) a term used in the New Testament, only (and without exception) when referring to Christians.

James' use of the word shows us without doubt that his epistle is written for Christian believers today. The reference to the twelve tribes scattered abroad was a reference to Christian Jews who had become a part of the Church *(ekklésia)*.

QUESTION 4 | *Why do we not see as many miracles in the West as in Africa and Asia?*

Having worked for many years in Africa and Asia, I believe a number of significant reasons stand out.

Firstly, we do not have their simple faith in God's Word. When we find a promise of God, we so often question, 'I wonder what He really meant?', rather than taking God at His Word.

There is a dependence on God that we in the West know very little of. As one Asian man recently said to me, 'When your people are sick they go straight to the doctors. It would cost me eight years' wages to be treated for my condition. If God does not heal me, I am dead'. So often we turn to God only when the doctors give up! Often it is then out of fear and desperation we pray, rather than out of faith.

Also we are so rational. From early on in life we are taught that north is always up and we form equally strong opinions on most other areas of life too. We have been taught to categorise the spirit world along with fairies and elves. This adversely affects us so that, even when we witness a miracle, there can be something inside us that says, 'there must be a natural explanation'.

As children we are taught that 'seeing is believing'. So, if you can see it, then it exists, but if you cannot see it, then it does not. We make a few exceptions of course, for things like radio waves. Why? Because scientists tell us that they exist and explain that this is where the sounds on our radios come from. It is amazing how most western Christians will far more readily accept the word of scientists than the Word of God. Receiving healing by faith, before we see immediate evidence, goes against our rational mind-set. Thus we often miss God's blessings which are received by faith.

Another problem is that we are so materialistic; everything revolves around this life. Most Christians believe that the acquiring of earthly possessions takes a higher priority than investing in the eternal and 'laying up treasures in heaven'. Our actions show this. Yet for many African and Asian believers they have little else in life but their faith in God.

We are also so humanistic, believing that human accomplishment is the real solution to the world's problems. For years preachers taught that with the advancement of medical science miracles were no longer required.

When encountering illness, most western Christians think of doctors and medicine before prayer. God is there when medicine fails!

I rejoice at all the great strides that medical science has made in its efforts to alleviate human suffering, yet isn't it amazing that with all our achievements we still have not found a cure for the common cold! Untold thousands are still not beyond the reach of a miracle. Man is not God.

It is sad that many Christians who have seen others healed and perhaps have received healing themselves, still find that they fight scepticism and unbelief. How we need to learn from the simple faith of our precious African and Asian brothers and sisters.

This unbelief must be dealt with before we can see a breakthrough of the miraculous.

However, things are changing. More and more, as we are standing on the Word of God, we are seeing miracles taking place in our land. I was recently speaking to a gathering of over 3,000 Christians in London and asked how many had ever received a miracle of healing from the Lord. Over three-quarters of the people raised their hand to say that they had.

QUESTION 5

But it's not scientific to believe in the miraculous, is it?

In the mid-seventeenth century, René Descartes introduced a mathematical concept of life that changed man's thinking in Europe. His teaching that 'all reality resulted from a mechanical cause and effect and could be explained scientifically' was radical. Descartes firmly believed in God and emphasised that it was impossible for God not to exist. Yet it was not long before his philosophy was adopted and God excluded.

Hence, we live in a society where God's existence is either denied or seen as largely insignificant. The world is viewed as a closed system, governed by the causes and effects of natural laws. Sadly, even in many churches, things are so well organised that we wouldn't notice if God hadn't turned up.

But in reality there is no tension between Christianity and science. Many of the greatest scientists have been convinced Christians. Faith and science are in fact complementary. In order for scientific discoveries to be made, many years of faith in a theory often precede any concrete evidence to convince anyone else. Science is often an exercise in faith. But ultimately we only believe what we want to.

A girl in America was healed of epilepsy, from which she had suffered for twenty years. During that time, drugs had been prescribed to control her symptoms. In addition to this brain 'defect', she had suffered from migraine headaches which no amount of medication had relieved. They had been so bad that she had missed months of schooling and been unable to hold down a regular job. As she was prayed for, she felt something happen. The next week E.E.G. tests to monitor her brain activity showed no signs of disturbance. The doctor concluded that the machine was malfunctioning and arranged another test.

The second test showed no signs of the previous illness either and so her medication was reduced. Further tests two weeks later showed no evidence of epilepsy and so her medication was discontinued.

After two years, with no further seizures or headaches, her doctors were still puzzled. The amazing thing is that they refused to believe her testimony that God had healed her. Their western view-point ruled out the possibility of Divine intervention. Rather, they concluded that she must have been mis-diagnosed and mistreated for the past twenty years. These conscientious doctors would rather risk being sued for malpractice, than admit the possibility of God having intervened!

QUESTION 6 | *What about the sceptics?*

The sceptical Pharisees requested a sign as proof of Jesus' identity, while ignoring the numerous signs that were already evident around them (Matthew 16:1–4).

Some will always refuse to believe. This should not surprise us. It was true even in Jesus' day. As one sceptical doctor put it on television recently, 'If after research I could find no explanation for the claimed miracle I would just conclude that the condition had been mis-diagnosed in the first place.'

We will never convince every sceptic. Even Jesus could not do that! If our philosophy of life excludes the miraculous, whatever God does we will refuse to acknowledge it.

Isn't it amazing that when Jesus healed a blind man, the Pharisees, rather than change their thinking, sought to kill the blind man to get rid of the evidence?

God's moving does not always make a preacher popular. During the 1970s, here in Britain, I was told by some pastors, 'We would support your evangelistic crusades if you would renounce praying for the sick.' Yet healing is a vital and inseparable part of the gospel which we have been sent to proclaim.

Jesus said; 'Go into all the world and preach the gospel to every creature...and these signs will follow them that believe; in My name they will cast out demons...they will lay hands on the sick and they will recover' (Mark 16:15–18).

In Mark's gospel, where Jesus' full commissioning is recorded, we see that laying hands on the sick, is included in Jesus' Great Commission before His ascension.

The accounts of the miracles shared in this book have all been confirmed by the crusade organisers before they were shared in print.

It is not our desire to share sensational stories, but genuine testimonies of what God has done. Honesty and integrity are vital, as I do not take lightly the blessing and favour of God on this ministry.

Yet, no matter how much care one takes, there will always be those who think that they can explain away what God has done. When things do not fit in with our philosophy or theology, rather than change our beliefs, we try to destroy the evidence.

Sometimes, of course, we have to take people's word that they have been healed, though the excitement and tears that usually flow are a sure indication that God has done something. People often write to us weeks, months and sometimes years later, confirming that a genuine miracle has taken place.

Those who regularly receive our *Reach Out Magazine* will know that the testimonies from our crusades around the world usually say that those whose eyesight had been healed (for example), testified that they had been blind but now could see. It is not our claiming that they were healed, it is their coming and telling us what God has done.

On some occasions, like a blind beggar who was healed in Tanzania, I have asked, 'How many knew this man and knew that he had been blind?'. Every hand in the crowd went up.

The same happened in Zimbabwe, where a deaf child was healed and a large group of his friends confirmed that he previously could not hear. Usually there are friends, neighbours and family members present to confirm the healings.

On one occasion I encouraged a husband to whisper 'I love you', in his wife's ear. She had been deaf in that ear since birth. The joy and tears that flowed as she threw her arms around him, saying, 'I love you too,' was proof enough that a miracle had taken place.

As one Muslim nurse recently put it after attending one of our missions, 'I didn't believe the reports I had heard. I did not believe these things could ever happen. But now I have seen it with my own eyes, I have to believe'.

This is one of the reasons that we try to video our crusades overseas. Many in our own land have never seen the blind receive their sight, the deaf hear and the lame walk. If we are to see such miracles here, we need to lift our faith.

Videos capture something of the excitement of what God is doing. Many sceptics have gone away convinced after attending our crusades.

An increasing number of Westerners are beginning to doubt the sufficiency of materialism and logic. There is a rapid rise of interest in the occult and in New Age religion. If the Church fails to bring its believing into line with the Word of God and experience God's miraculous power, we may well miss reaching this spiritually-hungry generation.

QUESTION 7 | *I received prayer but have not been healed. Why?*

People often ask, 'Why was I not healed?' Without divine revelation, of course, we cannot give a specific reason. There could be many hindrances and so it is good to search our hearts asking the Holy Spirit to show us if there are any. Past occult involvement can hinder receiving our healing, so can areas of sin in our life. Fear, anxiety and resentment can block the flow of God's healing too. If we are honest, unbelief often hinders the answers to our prayers. It is **not** for us to go around accusing others of unbelief, but it is good to search our own heart.

Some dear saints are not healed because of false teaching. Many believe that sickness and pain are sent by God to chasten them or to make them submissive to His will. So, amazingly, they have prayed for patience to be submissive to God's will instead of for healing. The irony is that many have then immediately called a doctor to give them medication. Is this submission to God's will? You will never be healed as long as you think that God wants you to be sick. Many precious saints cannot pray the prayer of faith to be healed, because they believe that it is God's will that they should be sick. With such false teaching having been so prevalent in the Church, it should not surprise us that many are not healed. However, things are changing and as we continue to stand on God's Word we will see more and more miracles.

Sometimes, however, after searching our heart to ensure that there is no sin or personal blockage to receiving healing we just have to hold on in faith. As we have seen, not everyone is healed instantly. In my own experience, most of the miracles I have received have been as I have stood on the promises of God and held on in faith until I have been completely healed.

I have covered this question and subject in much greater detail in my book, *Believing is Seeing*, available from Reach Out Ministries.

QUESTION 8 | *How does unbelief hinder answered prayer?*

I believe that the major hindrance to seeing miracles today is unbelief. Jesus said, 'Heaven and earth will pass away, but my words will by no means pass away' (Matthew 24:35). Yet Christians still so often doubt the Word of God and His promises.

Unbelief limited God moving in Jesus' own town: 'Jesus did not do many mighty miracles there because of their unbelief' (Matthew 13:58).

Mark's Gospel tells us 'He *could not* do any miracles there except lay his hands on a few sick people and heal them. And he was amazed at their lack of faith' (Mark 6:5,6).

Isn't it astonishing that the Bible tells us that there are things that the Son of God 'could not' do? If a preacher had said that, he would have been accused of being a heretic. But it is the Word of God that says it. Our unbelief hinders God moving.

God, of course, can do anything. He is a sovereign God. But in His sovereignty He has chosen to work in response to faith. As a sovereign God he has every right to do that.

Years of preaching that God does not perform miracles today or that we cannot expect Him to work miracles, has left an atmosphere of unbelief in our land which so often stops our prayers breaking through. The Word of God is clear. Jesus' miracles were not just God's sovereign intervention, doing whatever he liked. He responded to faith. Faith in the promises of God's Word is vital to receiving answers to our prayers (Mark 11:2, Matthew 21:21, Mark 9:23, Matthew 9:29).

When Jesus' disciples asked why they had been unable to cast the demon out of the child, Jesus said, 'because of your unbelief' (Matthew 17:20).

It is a waste of time praying for healing to 'see if it works'. The Bible tells us to 'ask in faith, with no doubting, for he who doubts is like a wave of the sea, driven and tossed by the wind. For let not that man suppose that he will receive anything from the Lord' (James 1:6,7).

For those who believe that the day of miracles is past, it is past. For Jesus said 'according to your faith let it be to you' (Matthew 9:29). Signs follow 'them that believe' (Mark 16:16–20).

There is an atmosphere of unbelief in many lands and churches which hinders our seeing the dynamic and supernatural move of God which, I believe, He wants us to see.

It is time to see that our unbelief is sin. Unbelief calls God a liar. It says, 'I know that you have said that you will do these things, but I do not believe that you will.' The **only** solution for sin is repentance. Then we can prayerfully go to God's Word, that faith might come to receive our healing.

QUESTION 9

We have started praying for the sick in our church but only a few have been healed so far. Why is this?

Sometimes few are healed, because pastors pray for the sick, but they do not preach boldly about Christ's healing power to build up people's faith to receive a miracle. I am sometimes asked by pastors, 'How do I start praying for the sick?' I usually reply, 'You don't. You start preaching to the sick first.' There is a **very** important principle here.

Thousands were healed in the meetings of F. F. Bosworth.

During his lifetime he received over 220,000 written testimonies from those who were miraculously healed. They used to take the wheelchairs and crutches away from his meetings by the truckload. Yet, during his crusades, he would preach for the first three days to build up people's faith before he would pray for anyone. He saw the necessity of dealing with people's unbelief and wrong beliefs (which led to their unbelief) first. He dealt with their nagging doubts about why they might not get healed before he prayed for any. He felt that otherwise they would come for prayer in unbelief and just go home disappointed, unhealed and blaming God.

Many pastors are fearful of boldly preaching God's Word on this subject. However, there has been so much negative preaching against miracles and healing, that if we do not destroy these wrong beliefs by preaching the positive truths of God's Word, we may as well not pray. It is the prayer of faith that saves the sick, not just prayer (James 5:15). We are told that the Lord confirms the Word with signs following (Mark 16:20). The Word must come first.

As the Word of God is preached on this subject and the people believe it, so faith comes to receive their healing. We must preach the Word of God in simplicity. If God says it, then He means it! The promises of God do not need interpreting, they need believing. The Bible was not written by learned theologians, nor was it written for theologians, it was written by simple believers, for simple believers.

I have a friend who has been mightily used by God all over the world in seeing tens of thousands saved and healed. Yet, before this fruitful ministry began, he had been a missionary who had not seen anyone won for Christ. One day God spoke to him and said, 'Why don't you preach My Word?' He said, 'Lord, I do preach Your Word. Every Sunday I preach Your Word'. God said, 'No you do not. You explain My Word, you talk about My Word, you interpret My Word. Why don't you just preach My Word?'

He began to boldly preach it, just as it is written. If He read; 'anything you ask in My Name I will do,' He began to preach that. Soon miracles began to happen and many started coming to Christ. The Lord has used him and his wife all around the world since then to see tens of thousands saved and healed.

Lots of Christians, when they are sick, head straight for the first healing line. Yet on most occasions in the New Testament, before Jesus healed people, most of them had heard Him preach. The usual pattern was to preach the Word and then to heal the sick. It is no use praying for people until their faith has been built up.

Many Christians, instead of saying 'Pray for me', should first say 'Teach me God's Word so that I can co-operate with God to receive a miracle'.

Before the Lord healed Lazarus, He said, 'Take away the stone' (John 11:38). That big round stone was like a giant full stop. 'Lazarus is dead [full stop].' Jesus said 'roll away the stone'. Notice Jesus did not take the stone away. It is our responsibility to get rid of our unbelief. We put it there by the books we have read and by the people and preachers that we have listened to, so we must get rid of it. Then, once the stone of unbelief has been rolled away, we can receive a miracle.

We need to recognise that unbelief is sin. It calls God a liar. It says 'I know that you have said that you will do these things, but I do not believe that you really will.' There is only one answer for sin and that is repentance.

We need to ask God to forgive us for our unbelief and to start to believe His Word.

However, on a positive note, things are changing. As the Church of Jesus Christ is opening more and more to this message of faith, so we are seeing more and more miracles taking place. I recently ministered at a series of meetings in England, where there were 2,000 people present. At the second meeting over 500 of those present acknowledged that they had been physically healed by the Lord in the previous meeting alone! England is not noted for its great faith!

QUESTION 10 — *Doesn't the Bible warn against the possibility of counterfeit miracles?*

Yes, it does. That is one of the reasons why we need to look at the doctrines of those ministering. Does the minister encourage you to put your faith in Jesus? Does he encourage you to believe and to study the Word of God? Are his teachings clear from reading the Word of God or do you need the preacher's 'special revelations' to maintain belief? Does he present Jesus as the healer or does he claim to have healing power of his own? The enemy is coming in like a flood and we must re-emphasise the centrality of Bible-based teaching.

Pharaoh's magicians were able to produce some miraculous demonstrations similar to those God performed through Moses. Therefore, any ministry that diverges from such foundational truths as the divinity of Christ, the all-sufficient sacrifice of Calvary and salvation by grace through faith should be rejected.

For example, spiritism is a counterfeit of true healing in Jesus' Name. The Bible clearly condemns attempts at contacting the dead (Deuteronomy 18:9–13). People go to spiritists looking for physical healing and end up spiritually bound. If you have ever been to a spiritist healer you need to repent and ask the Lord to set you free from the effects in Jesus' Name.

There is only one true healer and His Name is Jesus. Do not look to a man or woman to heal you. That is why Christians do not use the term 'faith healing'. It is 'divine healing' we believe in, for Jesus is the healer.

QUESTION 11 — *Isn't the desire for miracles a sign of ignorance?*

No, it rather reveals humanity's intense desire to know the reality of the unseen God. God's purpose and plan for humanity from the beginning was for people to have fellowship with Him.

Created in God's image, men and women can never find full satisfaction without Him. Human beings instinctively seek God, whether or not they admit it or are even conscious of it. Human life has divine purpose and until that purpose is discovered, there is a vacuum, an emptiness. Being the offspring of a miraculous God, people have an inborn hunger to experience miracles. This yearning for the miraculous is deep-seated in each human being regardless of nationality or background.

Jesus attracted the multitudes by miracles and wherever miracles are wrought in His Name today, He continues to attract the multitudes.

QUESTION 12

Some ministers and doctors have opposed divine healing because some of those who have come for prayer were disappointed. What is your reaction to this?

Not everyone who comes for prayer is healed instantly. We often have to hold on by faith before we receive. So, it would be foolish to judge the miraculous solely on the immediate results.

Also, let us not forget that doctors 'disappoint' millions every day. Nearly everyone in the graveyard has been to a doctor first. Some ministers who object to divine healing because some are not healed, do not minister to the sick themselves at all. That leaves everyone unhealed! Where is compassion or obedience to the scriptures in that?

A lot more are healed when we minister to the sick than when we do not!

QUESTION 13

Why do you say that God is on the side of health?

3 John 2 tells us: 'Beloved, I desire above all things that you might prosper and be in health, even as your soul prospers.'

God has even designed our bodies to be on the side of health. As soon as a germ enters our bodies, nature begins to repel it. When we break a bone or cut a finger, as long as our body is working properly, it does its utmost to heal and usually succeeds. Has God commanded our bodies to rebel against His will?

If sickness were the will of God, then every doctor would be in rebellion against Him and every nurse would be defying the Almighty. Every hospital would be a house of rebellion instead of a place of mercy. If sickness is the will of God then instead of supporting hospitals we should be seeking to close them down! But I believe that the Scriptures are clear that God is on the side of health.

QUESTION 14

Shouldn't we accept our sickness as a gift from God?

Such a fatalistic attitude can be found in Islam, Buddhism, Hinduism, and many other world religions, but not in the Bible.

Nowhere in Scripture do we find Jesus encouraging people to 'accept their sickness as a gift from God' or to 'bear it for His glory'. Nowhere do we find Jesus exalting 'the finer qualities' that can be developed through suffering illness.

Jesus never met sickness passively. He never regarded sickness as a friend to be welcomed, but as an enemy to be defeated. Jesus saw sickness as oppression by the devil and healed all who came in faith.

'God anointed Jesus of Nazareth with the Holy Spirit and with power, who went about doing good and healing all who were oppressed by the devil, for God was with Him' (Acts 10:38).

QUESTION 15

Jesus didn't heal all the sick in Israel, did He?

It is true that Jesus did not heal all of the sick in Israel, but there are no accounts of Him ever turning anyone away who came to Him in faith.

QUESTION 16 | *Doesn't God sometimes use sickness to discipline us?*

Sickness can result from our having sinned, but, when it does, it should last only as long as the sin continues.

Paul made it clear in the case of the sickness and death visited upon some of the Corinthian Church, that this was as a result of their sin (1 Corinthians 11:27–31). However, God's intention was not that the Corinthians should passively accept their sickness, but rather that they should stop sinning and be healed.

It was not God's will that these people were sick and had even died. It was His will that they should judge themselves, seek His forgiveness and receive healing. Neither was it God that had caused the sickness. Paul spoke of them as being 'handed over to Satan' for the destruction of their bodies that their souls might be saved. When we choose to walk in disobedience, we come out from under God's protective hand and place ourselves open to the attack of the enemy who is out to kill, to steal and to destroy.

When Jesus encountered the paralytic he did not tell him that this was God's discipline or preach a long accusing sermon about the man's sins. Instead He forgave the man and told Him to rise up and walk. To the man at the Pool of Bethesda Jesus said, 'Go and sin no more lest anything worse come to you' (John 5:14).

Some have taught that sickness is God's discipline in our lives, but a parent's discipline is only of value if the child knows what it is for. To repeatedly strike a child without explanation has no educational value but turns the child against the parent.

It is unreasonable to suggest that chronic illness is a form of discipline for a believer who, having searched his heart, honestly believes before God that there is no area of disobedience in his life.

What many Christians have called 'a blessing from God', would, in the human family, be called child abuse. What human mother or father would put cancer on their son or daughter to tame their pride?

Sickness is not from God.

The preachers who try to comfort the sick by telling them to accept their illness as a blessing from God, or say that God is trying to teach them a lesson, offer no consolation and certainly did not get this concept of sickness from Jesus!

QUESTION **17** *What do you think is the root of the concept that sickness is good for us and has a sanctifying effect?*

Roman persecution of the church stopped during the time of Constantine as the Church and State combined. This concerned many for they noted that as Christianity became the official religion of Rome its spiritual standards dropped. Many fled to the desert to practise asceticism concluding that without State persecution they would have to persecute themselves.

The ascetic behaviour of prolonged fasting, exposure to the elements, deprivation of sleep, flogging, etc., in some perverted way became synonymous with suffering for the faith. The Greek concept that divided body from spirit and concluded that the former was evil and should be degraded and rejected, crept into the Church. The warped concept that anything which hindered the body's comfort and pleasure, like sickness, was 'good for the soul', became more and more accepted.

Soon the notion of the sanctifying effect of sickness became firmly rooted in the Church. No longer was sickness seen as an enemy which should be defeated as it was in the practice of Jesus and His early disciples. Rather, the possible benefits of the sickness were emphasised. So much so that such commands as James 5:13–18 which encouraged prayer and the anointing of the sick that they might be made well, was exchanged for 'last rites'!

Instead of prayer being made that the sick person might be made well (James 5:15), it was seen that the 'healing' required was of the soul, in preparation for death.

In the sixteenth century the Church of England included these words in the office of visitation of the sick: 'Wherefore, whatsoever your sickness is, know you certainly that it is

God's visitation'. So engrained was this unbiblical concept that many of the New England Puritans opposed precautions against smallpox on the grounds that sickness was in God's providence and that to prevent it would thwart the will of God.

This unbiblical concept still continues for many in the Church today. It produces the common situation whereby Christians decline prayer for healing when they are sick concluding that it must be God's will that they are ill. Yet they still visit doctors and surgeons.

QUESTION 18 | *Doesn't the New Testament teach us that suffering is inevitable for the believer?*

The Bible teaches that faithful believers may well suffer persecution for his or her faith but suffering for the faith and physical sickness are never equated in the New Testament.

In the New Testament suffering always refers to persecution inflicted by people or demons. The Greek word translated in our English Bibles 'suffering' is *pascho*. There are sixty-five appearances of this word in the New Testament. On no occasion was it used in reference to sickness. The only reference to suffering in the context of anything physical is that of the epileptic, where the condition is attributed to a demon (Matthew 17:15). When it is used in Mark 5:26, 'the woman suffered many things' the term refers not to the woman's illness but to her treatment by the doctors!

Persecution may come to those who boldly proclaim Christ (Acts 4:1–22, 5:40–42, 7:54, 8:3, 14:19–20). This does not mean that we should not pray for deliverance from persecution; even the early Church did that (Acts 12:5). On occasions individuals were miraculously delivered, at other times they were not and endured their suffering with joy, rejoicing because 'they had been counted worthy of suffering disgrace for His Name' (Acts 5:41).

Though the English word 'suffer' may include the concept of sickness, in New Testament times it did not. Suffering and sickness were seen as very different from each other. Nowhere in the teaching or practice of Jesus did He promote sickness or counsel anyone that it was inevitable or profitable.

Nowhere did Jesus inflict sickness on anyone to accomplish some higher good, though He healed people for that reason (eg John chapter 9).

To Jesus sickness was an enemy not a friend. His response was to heal.

QUESTION 19 | *Should a Christian use doctors?*

I thank God for the medical profession. A number of my friends and supporters are doctors. Although several occult-rooted practices have recently crept in, like hypnotism and acupuncture, which are unacceptable for the believer, I am grateful to God for most of the medical discoveries man has made.

Doctors and nurses are on the side of health just as God is. 'Jesus answering said unto them, they that are whole need not a physician; but they that are sick' (Luke 5:31).

God heals in many ways, including through the treatment of doctors. I appreciate doctors because they believe in healing and that people should be well. Doctors are against disease, just as I believe God is. There are some sad and tragic stories of Christians who have taken a total stand against using medical science. I see no conflict between God's healing power through faith and prayer and the doctor's efforts to bring healing.

QUESTION 20 | *Should I give up my tablets now that I have been prayed for?*

Only the Lord can give that kind of directive. Ultimately, when you are physically well again you will not need them. The fact that you ask the question is perhaps an indication that this is not the right time to do so. The time to take such action is when you have complete peace in you heart that this is what God wants you to do, not when you have doubts about it. To do so without a clear directive from the Lord would be unwise. When the Lord is directing you to do something, you will have complete peace about it. It is the devil who tries to get us to do something out of condemnation. Although we want to take steps of faith, we also want to get our timing right and not to do anything that would damage our testimony. If the drugs are for a serious illness or have been taken for a prolonged period of time, it is good, if possible, to seek the counsel of a Christian doctor. As you seek the Lord, He can show you what is best, both for you and for His glory. It is just as exciting when a person has been healed and they find that they are getting a negative reaction from taking their medication or further medical tests show that their tablets are no longer required.

QUESTION 21

On what basis do some suggest that miracles and healing passed away on the death of the early apostles or on completion of the scriptures?

Having read books that object to the ministry of healing, I have not found one scriptural argument or one verse of Scripture mentioned that even suggests that miracles and healing would cease. The only verse that some have used to suggest that certain of the spiritual gifts would pass away is in 1 Corinthians 13:8 where we read: 'Whether there are prophesies, they will fail; whether there are tongues, they will cease; whether there is knowledge, it will vanish away'.

Are we suggesting that knowledge has passed away?

Verse 12 goes on to say; 'Now I know in part; then I shall understand fully, even as I have been fully understood'.

Has this happened yet?

Some suggest that this was a reference to the completion of the Canon of Scripture, yet at the time of writing Paul was not aware that at some future date his writings would be compiled with others to make the Scriptures. He was not referring to some prophetic event but to an event of which the Corinthian believers would be aware; a time when all the secrets of their hearts would be revealed and they would be seen and understood, as only God sees and understands. This is a verse which most believers see as a clear reference to the return of Jesus Christ.

Then, we will no longer need prophecy, which is for exhortation, edification and comfort (1 Corinthians 14:3). Encouraging, challenging and comforting will be a thing of the past. They are only required in this world of discouragement, apathy and pain. They will not be needed when we are with the Lord. They are however, vitally needed until then.

When Jesus comes, we will no longer need encouraging, exhorting and comforting. We will no longer need the gift of tongues (God's gift for wandering thoughts, mind blocks, uncertainty about how to pray, etc.) whereby we are enabled to pray beyond the limitations of our earthly language. Prayer will be replaced with praise for eternity. Then all our questions and disagreements within the body of Christ will be answered and we will know in full, in a way that we do not at this present time.

Nevertheless, even if this verse had meant that prophecy, tongues and knowledge would pass away prematurely, miracles and healing are not included in the list of those things that would pass away. This takes away the only verse that could be construed to imply an end to certain miraculous gifts. There is not one verse of scripture that even implies miracles or healing would cease.

Two streams of blessing flowed through the ministry of Jesus, a stream of forgiveness and a stream of healing. He came not just to save souls but to save people. He brought healing for the body and for the soul. These same two streams flowed side by side throughout the Book of Acts and on through Church history, with those who believed. Why should we suppose that one should run on until the Lord returns and the others fade away? There is no scripture to support such a concept.

As we have already seen, church leaders like Irenaeus, Luther, Zinzendorf, Wesley and Whitefield saw miracles of healing through their ministries. To suggest that miracles and healings stopped after the death of the early Church leaders or on completion of the Canon of Scripture is to dismiss the ministry of these great leaders.

If miracles have ceased, then we are all lost; for the greatest miracle that ever happens is when someone is born again.

It was not miracles that passed away but faith in God's power. When we stop preaching salvation, people do not get saved–when we stop preaching Christ's healing power, miracles cease. Today, however, when we will take God at His Word, we still see God's miracle power manifest.

Jesus said, 'Go into all the world and preach the gospel to every creature. He who believes and is baptised will be saved; but he who does not believe will be condemned. And these signs will follow those who believe: In My Name they will cast out demons; they will speak with new tongues; they will take up serpents; and if they drink anything deadly, it will by no means hurt them; they will lay hands on the sick, and they will recover' (Mark 16:15–18). This was our Lord's commission. Therefore, what right have we to preach only forgiveness and to withhold healing? What right have we to go to our world and demand acceptance of our message without signs following?

QUESTION 22

In your crusades you often, after prayer, encourage people to do what they could not do before. Why is this?

Faith without works is dead. Jesus told the blind man to 'go and wash in the pool of Siloam' (John 9:7). He encouraged the man to put actions behind his faith. The man was not healed until he did so. In the same way the Lord sent the ten lepers to show themselves to the priest. It was as they went that they were cleansed. None of them was healed at the point that they left Jesus.

In Acts chapter 3 we read that the lame man's feet and ankles were strengthened 'as he stood', not before he stood. He did not say 'I'm a lame man, I cannot stand!' He did not wait until he felt that something had happened. Many others, like that lame man, have received their healing as they have taken a step of faith and done what they could not do before.

QUESTION 23 | *Can psychological problems affect us physically?*

One prominent doctor recently said, 'four out of five times I would find out what was wrong sooner if I started by examining the patient's home-life, his job and his bank account instead of his heart, his digestive system and his kidneys'.

Dr Paul Tournier, the famous Swiss Physician, has often shared his beliefs that spiritual unrest, emotional trauma and damaged relationships lie behind most serious illnesses.

This should not surprise us, as the Bible frequently mentions the relationship between our body, mind and spirit (Psalm 38:3, Proverbs 3:5–8; 14:30). What goes on in one affects the others. When a person is prayed for and does not receive healing, it is often good to sit down and talk through with him or her whether there might be a root cause to their condition. It might be natural, spiritual, relational or emotional.

Discovering when the problem first started, whether there were any traumatic experiences around that time and whether sin or relational stress is a contributing factor can be helpful.

Learn to listen to God and to listen between the lines to what those you are counselling say. Many hurting people may know more about their problem than they are willing to admit, so gently encourage them to open up.

When there has been resentment or bitterness, forgiving the one who has offended often precedes healing.

The Bible links God's forgiveness of me with my forgiveness of others (Matthew 18:35; Luke 11:4). Often relationships need to be healed before our bodies can be healed. I have seen many people instantly healed when they have forgiven others.

It might also be worth mentioning, that Jesus once asked a man the question, 'Do you want to be healed?' This may seem like a strange question to someone who is sick. Yet, many sick people while appearing to moan about their sickness, at the same time hold onto it. Their sickness brings them the support and attention which they cannot face being without.

Negative attitudes, criticism and worry can ruin our health. Stress is a major killer in our society; it often leads to heart attacks, ulcers, high blood pressure and mental breakdowns. Jesus said, 'Never be troubled about tomorrow; tomorrow will take care of itself' (Matthew 6:34). He told us not to worry (Matthew 6:25,34). Yet, how many Christians ruin their health through fear, overworking and constant worrying? If we want to live in health, we need to learn to entrust our life and future, and the lives of our loved ones to the Lord.

Divine healing is more than just 'getting well'. It includes the healing of our emotions and a total healing of our relationships with God and with one another.

QUESTION 24 | *Should we not just pray 'Thy will be done?'*

It seems absurd to teach that, when it comes to areas of healing, Christians should pray as Christ prayed in the garden, 'Nevertheless, not My will, but Thine be done.' Jesus did not pray this prayer because He had any doubt concerning God's will. He never had a doubt about the matter. He prayed, 'If it is possible, let this cup pass from Me; nevertheless, not as I will, but as You will' (Matthew 26:39). This was His reaction in His humanity, to the awful prospect of the agony of the cross, to draw back. However, He knew that it was God's will that He should die for us in this way.

James 5:15 tells us 'the prayer of faith shall save the sick, and the Lord shall raise him'. It does not say 'and the prayer of faith shall save the sick if it be the Lord's will!' Since God does not insert this proviso when giving us this command to pray, why should we insert it? There is a proper time and place to insert 'if it be thy will' when we pray. James 4:13,15 tells us, 'Come now, you who say, "Today or tomorrow we will go to such and such a city, spend a year there, buy and sell and make a profit"; whereas you do not know what will happen tomorrow...Instead you ought to say, "If the Lord wills we will live and do this or that".' It is in the area of our future plans for which there is no clear scriptural directive that we are told to add 'if the Lord wills'.

It is such plans as whether to move, to take certain business opportunities, etc., that we ought to pray and say, 'Lord, I only want to do what you want me to do'. It is in such human plans, where there is uncertainty of God's will, that such a prayer has its rightful place, not in the areas where God's Word is clear concerning His will.

When we inject the proviso 'if it be thy will' concerning healing, it is an acknowledgement that we are not praying the prayer of faith but that we have doubts in our own hearts. James warns us to 'Ask in faith without doubting. For he that doubts is like the waves driven and tossed about. Let not that man suppose that he should receive anything from the Lord' (James 1:7).

When we pray in faith Jesus tells us to believe that we have already received that for which we have prayed. Such a prayer cannot be offered unless we are first convinced from God's Word that it is His will to heal us.

QUESTION 25 | *If it is God's Will to heal me, won't it just happen?*

If someone said to you, 'I don't need to give my life to Christ. God knows whether I am going to be saved or lost anyway,' you would call this fatalism not faith. You would explain to him that to be saved he must meet God's condition for salvation by believing in the Lord Jesus Christ.

In the same way, when we pray for the sick inserting the words 'if it be thy will' we are placing all of the responsibility for that healing on to God and assuming none for ourselves. The scriptures, however, place the responsibility on our shoulders. Jesus said, 'And all things, whatsoever you ask in prayer, *believing,* you will receive' (Matthew 21:22).

In Mark 9:22 the father of a demon-possessed boy said to Jesus 'If You can do anything, have compassion on us, and help us'. Christ replied, 'If you can believe, all things are possible to him who believes'. The father then replied, 'Lord, I believe: help Thou my unbelief'.

Christ let the father know that the 'if', the responsibility for healing, did not lie with God but with the father himself.

God puts the responsibility for answered prayer on us. 'And Jesus answering said unto them, "Have faith in God. For verily I say unto you, that whoever shall say unto this mountain be thou removed, and be thou cast into the sea, and shall not doubt in his heart, but shall believe that those things which he sayeth shall come to pass: he shall have whatever he sayeth. Therefore I say unto you, whatsoever things you desire, when you pray, believe that you receive them, and you shall have them" ' (Mark 11:22–24).

To the blind men Jesus said, 'Do you believe that I am able to do this? According to your faith be it done unto you' (Matthew 9:29). To the centurion, Jesus said, 'Go your way and as you have believed, so it will be done unto you' (Matthew 8:13). To the woman with the issue of blood Jesus said, 'Daughter, your faith has made you whole; go in peace and be whole of your plague' (Mark 5:34). To Jairus who came on behalf of his little daughter, Jesus said, 'Be not afraid, only believe' (Mark 5:36). It was when Jesus 'saw their faith' that He healed the paralytic carried to Him by the man's friends.

QUESTION 26 | *Are there not spiritual benefits from being sick?*

Some have had 'deep spiritual experiences' during times of confinement, for which we can praise God. But, should it be necessary to experience such things to draw us closer to the Lord?

For every believer who speaks of having had such a 'deep spiritual encounter', there are many more who have been constantly occupied with themselves, with careful eating, with taking their tablets on time, with ensuring that they receive sufficient visitors, etc.

There are many beneficial lessons that we can learn as we

hold on in faith for our healing. However, a common problem with the view expressed in the question is that sickness is spiritualised, which stops many believers from reaching out to receive healing from Christ.

If there are the benefits that many suggest, then why didn't Jesus counsel people to stay sick? Why did He heal everyone who came to Him in faith?

QUESTION 27 | *Why do we need healing services?*

I have found God's presence to be very evident at such gatherings, when believers unite together in expectant faith. It is there that many are healed. For lots of people, such services have been among the greatest spiritual events that they have ever attended.

Secondly, there are too many people needing healing to try and minister to them all one by one. Jesus frequently healed *en masse*.

Thirdly, there is the public witness value of a large healing meeting. In an age when many doubt the power of prayer for healing, it is vital to have such visible healing meetings.

On almost every occasion Christ preached and healed in public (ie Matthew 8:16; 9:35; Mark 1 & 2). He also told His disciples to preach and to heal in public (Matthew 10:6–8; Luke 10:1–12). This continued throughout the Book of Acts. In Part Two of this book we will see that the mighty miracles that took place, were the reason that the crowds gathered. It was the miracles which caused the people to follow Christ and which led to most of the growth of the early Church (see Appendix 3).

We cannot improve on Jesus' way of ministering. I believe that much of the failure on the mission fields in reaching those of other religions, has been the lack of evidence of God's power. Paul said, 'My speech and my preaching were not with persuasive words of human wisdom, but in demonstration of the Spirit and of power, that your faith should not be in the wisdom of men but in the power of God' (1 Corinthians 2:4,5).

Multitudes turn to Christ in our crusades around the world on seeing the miracles of those that are healed.

QUESTION 28

Why do you often pray for people en masse *in your crusades?*

I find that ministering in this way encourages people to look to the Lord Jesus to heal them instead of looking to me. Jesus said of believers: 'They will lay hands on the sick and they will recover.' I often encourage the believers to lay their own hands on the ailing area of their body. Both at home and abroad I have found this to be one of the most effective ways of ministering healing.

I personally could pray individually for around 100 sick people in an evening after ministering the Word. On the other hand by praying from the platform I can pray for thousands at the same time and see many hundreds healed.

QUESTION 29

Do you often ask the congregation to lay hands on one another?

Rarely. Though I want to encourage Christians to step out in ministry, often I have felt that it has been very unwise when the leadership of a gathering has encouraged all the Christians to turn around and start laying hands on one another. Personally I am very cautious whom I allow to lay hands on me. Just as healing and wholeness can be imparted through the prayer of faith from the servant of God, so I believe that negative things can be imparted, for example, from one who has never repented of past occult involvement, if the one who is prayed for is not walking in faith and holiness. At one event I was involved in, I noticed two women present who were laying hands on everyone they could, at every opportunity they could. I discerned that something was not right. It became evident a few nights later when one of the ladies brought a 'prophecy' that the Lord would be returning in September! When the 'prophecy' was corrected the woman became very angry, and informed us that she was God's prophet. When I spoke to her later she claimed to regularly contact the dead. A few weeks later she ran off with another woman's husband. In large gatherings, how can we be sure that there are not witches, spiritists or members of the cults present? In such free gatherings there are liable to be many who lay hands on others and pray in doubt or make fleshly requests. Leaders need to protect the flock. Let me add, having shared this caution, that we do want to see the body of Christ mobilised and that wonderful things do happen when Christians pray for one another. This is where training others in ministry is so vital.

QUESTION 30

What about those who come with high expectations and leave in the same state of ill-health in which they came?

Let me first say that such meetings are still vital for those who are healed. Also, if handled wisely by the preacher, everyone can go home having met with the Lord afresh, rather than disappointed.

Enthusiastic preaching is vital at such services. However, wisdom and integrity are also needed from the preacher, so as not to suggest to the people that everyone who comes for prayer will be healed instantly. This kind of preaching can leave any who are not healed, either feeling resentful against God or guilty that it is solely because of their unbelief. We have seen that even in the Bible not everyone was healed instantly. Sometimes we just have to hold on in faith for our healing. This needs saying to encourage those who are in that position.

We cannot say, 'Everyone who comes for prayer tonight will be instantly healed.' We have already seen that Jesus was hindered by unbelief. Every meeting I have attended in the West has included those with a lot of faith, those with a lot of unbelief and those in between.

Nevertheless, I would rather major on the positive side of faith. Most of us have been present at gatherings where one of the ministers present wanted to inject 'reason' and 'balance' into the occasion. Yet his theological discourses just flattened the occasion.

Faith-filled preaching is vital. If the preacher has the right spirit and wisdom, he can lead everyone in the congregation to blessing at some level, including healing.

I would also add that we must never despise those who have not yet received their healing. Unfortunately I have heard people say critically to very sick or disabled Christians, 'If you had faith you would have been healed.' On several occasions I have turned to those people and said, 'Why don't you use your faith to get them healed?' The gospel is 'good news'. The message of healing brings hope. We must ensure that we share these truths to lift people's faith and not to condemn them.

Back in the early 1970s when the Lord filled me with the Holy Spirit it was not that common in Britain to hear about miracles in the mainline denominations. In that situation it would have been easy to have watered down the message of healing and to preach a theology of experience. We could have preached that it is not God's will to heal many people, because few were being healed. But that is no solution. It is only as we preach the Word of God and build people's faith that we will see more blessing.

It is now more common for people to be healed. At a recent meeting in Wembley Conference Centre I asked the crowd to raise their hand if they had ever been miraculously healed by the Lord. I was amazed to see that well over three-quarters of the hands were raised. Had I asked that same question of the crowd fifteen years ago, there would have been very few hands raised. In my African and Asian crusades it is very rare that anyone who comes for ministry is not healed. But, then they have not had years of doubt-filled preaching that God might not heal them.

Hebrews 11:13 speaks of those who 'died in faith, not having received the promises but, having seen them afar off, were assured of them, embraced them and confessed that they were strangers and pilgrims on the earth.' Some have died in faith, still standing on the promises. It is those situations, where we have believed and done all that we can, that we just have to entrust things to the Lord, that He knows best. However, for me there can be no greater blessing than standing on the promises of God. I want to go to the grave believing in the healing power of Christ, unless Jesus comes first! For I know that as God is dealing with the unbelief in our land, so we are seeing more manifestations of His miraculous power.

Apart from the challenge of standing on God's promises, there is something powerful and important in having faith and expectation. The devil wants us to give up fighting our sickness. When a person gives up hope it is very rare that they recover. I once read an article by a leading cancer researcher and surgeon where he said, 'I do not like to perform surgery on someone who is low in their spirit. I know that a person with an attitude like that has a much more difficult time surviving surgery and takes a much longer time in recovery.' When our faith is high the devil finds it far more difficult to attack us. A negative attitude will destroy our faith.

QUESTION 31 *Why do you say that a negative attitude will destroy our faith?*

God has given faith to everyone (Romans 12:3). Unbelief, along with negative thinking and speaking are not the results of a lack of faith. Rather they are using the faith that God has given us to believe for negative things to happen or to believe that God will not heal us and that his promises are unreliable. Faith is believing that God tells the truth and will do what He says He will do.

We need to see that a negative attitude is not a lack of faith, but it is wrong believing. Some people say, 'Its January, I'm bound to get a cold, I always do', or 'Arthritis (or any other disease) runs in the family. My mother had it, so I guess I will get it too.' Others say, 'My father died of cancer (or had a weak heart), so I probably will.' They believe that negative things will happen and in fact use their capacity for faith to get sick.

If you have had those kind of attitudes, ask God to forgive

you for wrong believing and stop entertaining such thoughts. They are things the devil wants you to expect and to believe. Such believing will pull you down and paralyse you spiritually. In faith, cut yourself off from the effects of all hereditary diseases. Stand against them in Jesus' Name.

QUESTION 32 | *Were miracles limited to the apostles?*

No, Stephen and Philip were involved in the practical responsibilities of the Church (Acts 6:1–7). Yet we read, 'Stephen a man full of faith and power, did great wonders and signs among the people' (Acts 6:8). Of Philip we read, 'The multitude with one accord heeded the things spoken by Philip, hearing and seeing the miracles which he did. For unclean spirits, crying with a loud voice, came out of many who were possessed: and many who were paralysed were healed' (Acts 8:6,7).

Philip and Stephen were as gloriously used as Peter and John.

1 Corinthians 12:9 speaks of 'the gifts of healings', given as endowments to the church and there is no implication that these gift would cease.

James wrote at a time when many of the apostles had already lost their lives: 'Is any sick among you? Let him call for the elders of the church and let them pray over him, anointing him with oil in the Name of the Lord: and the prayer of faith shall save the sick and the Lord shall raise him up; and if he has committed sins, they shall be forgiven him' (James 5:14,15). Notice to whom he commits this directive–not just to apostles or to a few men and women of rare gifts, but to the church elders, to those most likely to be within reach of every sufferer.

Jesus simply said of all believers, 'These signs will follow them that believe; in My Name they will cast out demons; they will speak with new tongues... they will lay their hands on the sick and they will recover' (Mark 16:17,18).

The thing that initially held me back from praying for the sick, was the nagging doubt that nothing might happen.

People did not begin to be healed until I decided that even if nothing happened, I was going to be obedient to my Lord.

Rather than limit these things to a few apostles, Jesus says of everyone who has faith, 'I tell you the truth, anyone who has faith in me will do what I have been doing. He will do even greater things than these, because I am going to the Father' (John 14:12 NIV).

QUESTION 33 | *I am a pastor. How do I start praying for the sick to be healed?*

First, start to preach on Christ's healing power and then offer at the close of the service to pray for people.

I first started praying for the sick because it is a command of Christ and not because people got healed. Most of us were praying for the sick for a while before we saw miracles take place. So, don't get discouraged. As you lift people's faith, more and more will be healed.

Invite preachers to your church who are used by the Lord to see the sick healed, both to support what you are sharing and to help lift people's faith. Read faith-building books and attend conferences and meetings where the sick are being healed to lift your own faith.

We read in 2 Corinthians 1:20, 'For all the promises of God in Him are yes, and in Him amen, to the glory of God through us.' If we find a promise in God's Word it is 'yes'. We do not have to ask God whether He means it. He has already said 'yes'. Let us not be frightened of the Bible or to preach God's Word boldly.

When Jesus said of those who believe that we would do greater things than He did, we might say, 'Well it's not happening in my experience.' Yet, does that mean that the Word of God is wrong? No, it means that our experience needs to change. We must start to take God at His Word, for God cannot lie (Hebrews 6:18). God is not unscriptural. Jesus said that 'Heaven and earth will pass away, but my words will by no means pass away' (Matthew 24:35). Unbelief says, 'I know you promised it, but I don't think you will do it.'

As we learn to stand on God's promises, so our faith will

rise and we will see more miracles. So, keep holding on and standing on the promises. Begin to take steps of faith.

QUESTION 34 | *What is my responsibility when it comes to living a healthy life?*

While focusing on God's ability to heal, we must not forget our own responsibility in caring for the body which God has entrusted to us.

God expects us to take care of our body. A good balanced diet, exercise, avoiding over-eating, learning to relax and getting sufficient sleep, are vital to living in health. Rest and relaxation are also important. As one doctor put it, 'In the treatment of nervous disease, we are now constantly compelled to prescribe periods of rest. Such periods are, I think, only Sundays in arrears.'

Often during my Crusades in Africa people request prayer for stomach disorders. To many, it would seem unspiritual, when they are seeking a touch from the Lord, to point out to them that if they would boil their water before drinking it, many of these problems would not occur.

Many of the Old Testament laws related to hygiene and were to keep Israel healthy.

We know that being grossly overweight can cause all kinds of physical problems and illnesses. Continually living under stress and anxiety or being controlled by competitiveness makes us prone to heart problems and heart attacks. Living with deliberate sin in our lives puts us under a psychological pressure that will often lead to sickness too.

Some doctors have told us that resentment can destroy the body's natural fluids and lead to arthritis. Because we are made up of body, soul and spirit, what goes on in my soul (my mind, my will and my emotions) will automatically affect my body.

Sometimes when we are sick we need to stop and to review our lifestyle to see if there is any disorder in our lives. Our bodies can sometimes work as an early warning system. Yet, with God's help we can change wrong lifestyle patterns and live in health.

QUESTION 35 — *Can I be prayed for again for the same condition, as I've been prayed for before?*

There is encouragement in the account of Jesus ministering to one blind man, for he was not instantly healed (Mark 8:22–26). There was an improvement, but he basically said, 'I can see clearer; I can see men, but they are like trees walking'. His eyesight was still blurred. So Jesus ministered to him a second time and he was made completely whole.

If there was an occasion when Jesus needed to minister a second time to someone, then how much more on occasions with us. The important thing is that those who receive further ministry come not, 'to see if it works this time,' but because their faith has been renewed for healing.

There is a time, as in Jesus' parable of the importunate widow, when we should keep asking and knocking in faith until we receive. As we are sensitive to the Lord's voice, He will show us when to keep asking and when to stop asking and to rest and receive by faith.

QUESTION 36 — *I thought I was healed, but my former symptoms have started to return. What should I do?*

On occasions, after a period of enjoying health, the first symptoms have appeared to return. It is then that many Christians move into unbelief. 'I thought I was healed', they say, 'I guess I must have been wrong.' Don't accept anything that the devil uses to attack you. Don't allow unbelief to open the door for the devil. Just because God has healed you does not mean that the devil will leave you alone. He will still try to put sickness on us, in the same way that he still tempts us after we have experienced God's victory in some area of our life.

One big problem is that some Christians receive healing on the faith of others (for example, the preacher's) but do not themselves have a foundation of faith in God's Word. So when those other people are not around to hold them up, they begin to doubt and to get into unbelief.

Often the devil tries to take people's healing. Instead of rising up and standing against him, they give in and say 'I guess God didn't heal me', because they have no foundation in the Scriptures.

We must learn to stand in faith on the Word of God. The Bible tells us, 'Above all take the shield of faith.' Just as new converts need to be established in the Word if they are to go on, so those who are healed need to be established in the Word.

Many Christians come for prayer for healing and almost as soon as they leave the meeting, they begin talking about their sickness as if they had not received ministry.

Often I have found that as I have continued to stand in faith, the devil gives up after a while, knowing that he cannot win! The Bible tells us to resist the devil and that he will flee (James 4:7). Some Christians seem to be waiting until a red fellow with a long tail and horns appears. The devil is more subtle than that, he comes in the form of doubt, fear, temptation, sickness and disease. It is these fears, doubts and sicknesses that we must resist in Jesus' Name. Jesus warned us that the devil is out to steal, but don't let him. Don't fall back into unbelief. Keep holding on!

QUESTION 37

Sometimes people use the word of knowledge to share details of people present that the Lord wishes to heal. Why is that?

When someone receives a word of knowledge for another about their condition, their faith rises to receive the word. It is not that God is more willing to heal them than others but, just an encouragement to their faith. Many times in meetings, I have noticed that there are sick people who do not come for prayer, mainly because they have no real conviction that God is going to heal them. Those are the ones that I usually get words of knowledge for. After receiving the word, their faith is released that God does want to do something. It is biblical, for Ananias received a word concerning Paul's need of healing (Acts 9:10–19) and even the address at which he was staying. It is one of the gifts of the Holy Spirit recorded in 1 Corinthians 12:4–11.

QUESTION 38

My pastor says that certain parts of the Bible are not for today. Is that so?

Who are we to decide which parts are for today and which parts are not? If God has changed His mind concerning healing, could He not have changed His mind about Heaven? To question one part of God's Word puts a question mark over it all.

The Bible gives a very clear warning against adding to or taking from God's Word.

If certain parts are not for today, you may as well get your scissors and cut them out. Why waste your time reading them? The problem is that some Christians would be left with very little more than the cover and the maps!

The truth is that God is unchanging and so is His Word. Heaven and earth will pass away but God's Word will never pass away (Matthew 24:35).

QUESTION 39

Do we first need to receive our miracle by faith before we see it?

Before Jesus called Lazarus from the tomb He prayed: 'Father, I thank you that you have heard me' (John 11:41). We can receive things by faith before the answer becomes visible. 'Faith is the evidence of things hoped for, the certainty of things not seen' (Hebrews 11:1). The Word of God tells us that faith receives from God, before anything visible is manifested.

Jesus tell us to believe that we have 'received' and then we will have our request (Mark 11:24).

Long before Sarah became pregnant, God said to Abram, 'The Father of many nations I have made you' (Genesis 17:5). Notice God was speaking in the past tense 'I have made'. In the same way Abram acted by faith, taking on his new name

'Abraham', which means the father of a multitude, even prior to Isaac's birth.

In receiving healing, faith rejoices and says 'it is written', before there is any physical change. It stands on the Word of God. Faith ceases to be anxious about the condition of our body, because we have committed it to the Lord and believe that He has heard. Many Christians, for example, have been healed after reading the words 'by his stripes we are healed' in Isaiah 53:5 and 1 Peter 2:24. Suddenly they have seen the past tense of this promise and declared, 'Lord, you said I am healed. I am going to believe it'. Our feelings often have to catch up with our faith.

In the period between God's promise to Abraham and its fulfilment, Abraham did not watch his symptoms and cast away his confidence because there was nothing visible to encourage him. He did the exact opposite and looking at the promise of God, 'he did not waiver at the promise of God through unbelief, but was strengthened in faith, giving glory to God' (Romans 4:20).

For twenty-five years he stood on the Word of God before he received his son. Many have been healed by standing on the promises of God concerning healing, in the same way that millions of sinners have been saved by standing on the promises of God's Word concerning forgiveness.

QUESTION 40

What about those who prayed in faith and yet did not recover and some that have even died?

Although we recognise God's limitless power, we still live in a fallen world where the whole of creation, including the human body, is 'subject to decay' (Romans 8:21). It will continue to be so until we receive our resurrection bodies (8:23). Although we enjoy the blessings of all that Jesus has accomplished on the cross, the **full** manifestation of Christ's victory will be seen when He returns.

When our prayers are not answered in the way that we had hoped they would be, we should not look for someone to accuse, rather we should remember that hope stands alongside faith. As Thomas Smail puts it in his book *Reflected Glory*, 'Hope has to do with God's promises that are still future and hidden, just as faith has to do with God's promises that are here and now. To the person who has believed for today, but has not seen the answer come today, comes the call of hope. Hope says, 'tomorrow is also God's. Enough has happened already to assure you that the rest is on the way'.

We believe that Jesus is coming again and that in heaven there will be no more suffering, pain, sorrow or dying. Until then we live in the situation where, even though Jesus raised people from the dead, they still later died. Yet for the believer, death is not the end and is in fact ultimate healing.

It would be foolish for those of us involved in healing ministries to speak as though there was never a time when people died. Let us not forget that even people like Lazarus, whom Jesus raised from the dead, eventually died. The glorious truth for the believer is that death is not the end but is just passing into the full presence of Jesus. The apostle Paul wrote, 'We are confident, yes, well pleased rather to be absent from the body and to be present with the Lord' (2 Corinthians 5:8). To the believer death is promotion not defeat. Even before the doctor has signed our death certificate, the King of Kings has taken us into God's presence.

One of the precious old saints at the turn of the century was J. C. Bevington. He once wrote; 'A man said to me some time ago, "Well, Brother Bevington, I suppose, from your teaching, that you are never going to die, as you say that God heals and that He answers prayer. So all that you have to do is pray, and He heals you." I reminded him of an incident that occurred while I was working at the carpenter trade near Michigan City, Indiana. As we were coming home one Saturday evening, in the buggy, we noticed a man and his wife walking around an old log house. They seemed to be scrutinising the old frame closely and as we came near, the man shouted "Hey Jerry, come in here". So when Jerry got out of the buggy, the man said, "My wife and I have been examining our old house where we have lived and raised our family of eleven. They are all gone now, married off. You know you have been fixing this old house up for us every year for several years. So we want you to build us a new house". We built one, and saw them vacate the old building and move in to the new. I said, "Sir, that is the way it will be with me, as Christ has promised to keep this building that I am living in, in repair; the time is coming and I expect soon to see Him come down, take a walk around this old frame and say 'Well, Bevington, now is the time to vacate it and move up here into the new mansion that we have just finished for you.' " '

Any message on healing which cannot bring comfort at the death bed, is not the good news of Jesus Christ. To the Christian, death is not defeat, but ultimate victory. Thus, we continue to pray in faith and can be confident that even when our prayer is not answered the way that we had hoped and expected it to be, resurrection bodies await all those who die in Christ. Because of Christ's victory at Calvary, death for the believer is no longer defeat.

We still await Christ's return. The battle against the forces of darkness still continues. One day soon however, we will receive our resurrection bodies (see 1 Corinthians 15). Until then our command and commission is as real today 'to preach the Kingdom of God and to heal the sick' (Luke 9:2) as it was when Jesus spoke those words 2,000 years ago.

For further reading, see Peter Gammons' book *Believing is Seeing*, available from Reach Out Ministries, PO Box 130, Walton On Thames, Surrey, KT12 2RU, England.

PART TWO

SEVEN REASONS WHY WE NEED MIRACLES TODAY

8 Miracles Are an Inseparable Part of the Gospel

'I do not come from a church background that emphasises healing. In fact, we have been a bit critical of it. Yet in my research I have discovered the winning of the lost has come in great numbers where men and women were healed in Christ's Name and amazing church growth has resulted. The evidence I uncovered in country after country – and in North America as well – simply wouldn't permit me to hold my former point of view. And I may say that as I meditated on it, my biblical conviction also wouldn't permit it. In other words, God is not helpless today. It is ridiculous to assume the only way He can heal is through injections or operations. As I have been reviewing church growth around the world I have seen that it frequently correlates with great healing campaigns.'

Donald A McGavran, Professor of Church Growth

Dr McGavran came to the above conclusion after spending fifty years of his life researching the subject of church growth world-wide.

During one of our crusades in Tanzania, a little boy was brought for prayer by his Muslim grandmother. He had been dumb from birth and had a paralysed left arm. I looked at the sad wizened face of the old woman who had brought him and the black religious gown in which she was dressed.

'In Jesus' Name, be healed!'

Immediately the boy began to move his previously limp arm and hand. He began to smile and then to squeeze my hand excitedly. I told my interpreter to tell the lad to repeat what I said.

'*Asante*,' I said slowly and clearly, which means 'Thank you'.

'*Asante*,' the boy replied, a glowing smile on his face as he spoke his first ever word.

'*Asante, Jesu*,' I continued.

'*Asante, Jesu*,' the boy replied.

The old woman wept with joy and the crowd got very excited.

The next morning, when I arrived at the church to hold a leader's seminar the old woman was already there, waiting for me. 'I want to know the Jesus who healed my grandchild,' she said.

I explained that she would have to give her whole life to Christ. Eagerly she agreed, saying, 'It was Jesus who healed the child.' We led her to Christ there and then.

That night she turned up at the meeting with a beautiful smile on her face, and a white gown with flowers all over it. She came up and handed me the potions, given her by the witch-doctor, saying, 'I don't need these anymore.'

Although it was not a massive crusade, over three thousand responded to receive Christ in twelve days. Months later I was still receiving letters from churches all over the area who had received hundreds of new members.

Jesus is the same today. His power has not changed.

Christians have discovered the power of the cross and of the resurrection. Many have discovered the power of Pentecost too. Yet very few seem to have grasped the significance of the ascension.

We fail to see that Jesus ascended back to Heaven and poured out the Holy Spirit so that we would continue on an ever-widening scale, what He had began. Jesus went back to

His Father and poured out the Holy Spirit, so that His work might expand, not decrease.

How often do we hear such statements as, 'I know that Jesus would heal me if He were here now'? Yet Scripture tells us that He is here now and His power has not changed. Jesus said, 'I will never leave you nor forsake you. Lo, I am with you always, even to the end of the age' (Matthew 28:20).

During His earthly ministry, Jesus was limited to being in one place at one time, but now He is not. He has poured out His Holy Spirit so that we can continue what He began.

> 'Do you not know yourselves, that Jesus Christ is in you?' (2 Corinthians 13:5, Galatians 2:20, Ephesians 3:17, Colossians 1:27)

The same Holy Spirit dwells in us as empowered the Lord Jesus in His ministry.

The statement, 'I know that Jesus would heal me if He were here now,' shows that we have failed to understand the ascension.

Luke, the writer of the Book of Acts, opens his account of the Lord's ongoing ministry through the early Church by referring to 'all that Jesus *began* both to do and teach' (Acts 1:1).

Christ's work was far from finished when He ascended back to His Father. Rather, it had just begun. The same Jesus who said, 'The Spirit of the Lord is upon Me, because He has anointed Me to preach the gospel to the poor. He has sent Me to heal the broken hearted, to preach deliverance to the captives and recovery of sight to the blind, to set at liberty those who are oppressed, to preach the acceptable year of the Lord' (Luke 4:18,19), has anointed us to continue the work He began and says, 'He who believes in Me, the works that I do he will do also; and greater works than these he will do, because I go to My Father' (John 14:12). Do we believe Him?

Jesus did not say that these 'greater works' were limited to His early disciples or to some select group of believers, but simply, 'he who believes'. That includes you.

Let us then consider the first of seven reasons why we need miracles today.

MIRACLES ARE AN INSEPARABLE PART OF THE GOSPEL

The grand reason why the miraculous gifts were so soon withdrawn, was not only that faith and holiness were well nigh lost, but that dry, formal, orthodox men began even then to ridicule whatever gifts they had not themselves, and to decry them all as either madness or imposture.

John Wesley *Journals*

How often have ministers written off miracles and healing as 'side issues'? 'We must not get side-tracked from our real call to proclaim the gospel and to see souls saved,' they say.

Yet Jesus spent a large part of His ministry healing the sick and setting captives free. How dare we call such things 'side issues'? To do so implies that Jesus was side-tracked in his ministry. We go out to save souls; Jesus wants to put the soul back in the body and 'save' the whole person!

To question the importance of miracles is to question a major part of Christ's ministry.

> And Jesus went about all the cities and villages teaching in their synagogues, preaching the gospel of the Kingdom, and healing *every* sickness and *every* disease among the people. Matthew 9:35

> Great multitudes followed Him and He healed them *all*. Matthew 12:15

> When evening had come, they brought to Him many who were demon possessed. And He cast out the spirits with a word and healed *all* who were sick. Matthew 8:16

> When the sun was setting, all those who had anyone sick with various diseases brought them to Him and He laid hands on *everyone* of them and healed them. Luke 4:40

> The whole multitude sought to touch Him for power went out from Him and healed them *all.* Luke 6:19

'As many as touched Him were made well' (Matthew 14:36) and He has not changed! Jesus Christ is 'the same yesterday, today and forever' (Hebrews 13:8). Jesus said, 'I have come down from heaven, not to do My own will, but the will of Him who sent Me' (John 6:38). He said that He and His Father were one (John 10:30) and that to know Him was to know the Father (John 8:19). If you have ever doubted what God's will is concerning healing, look at Jesus. He came to show us what God is like!

Healing and deliverance are a manifestation of the Kingdom. Jesus never sent His disciples to preach and not to heal. Healing the sick was as clear a command as baptising disciples.

Miracles were not just to 'prove who Jesus was'. They did not decrease at all after Jesus ascended to His Father, rather they increased (Acts 3:1–14; 8:5–8; 14:3; 28:8,9; 2 Corinthians 12:12; Galatians 3:5; James 5:14,15).

> Through the hands of the Apostles many signs and wonders were done among the people. Acts 5:12

> A multitude gathered from the surrounding cities to Jerusalem, bringing sick people and those who were tormented by unclean spirits and they were *all* healed. Acts 5:16

The message of Christ has suffered great damage through the efforts of some ministers and theologians, who, to excuse their own spiritual impotence, have relegated the supernatural to some transitional period in the first century. Yet deep within the hearts of men and women who love God's Word is a longing to rescue the Book of Acts from becoming no more than a history book and to put it back in its proper place, as a pattern for the church today. Miracles and healing are a vital and inseparable part of the gospel.

In his book *Christ the Healer*, F. F. Bosworth says, 'Instead of the ministry of healing diverting from the more important matter of salvation for the soul, we have seen more conversions in a single week than we ever saw in a whole year of evangelistic work during the thirteen years before the Lord led us to preach this part of the gospel in a bolder and more public way.'

9 THE GOSPEL IS NOT JUST A PROCLAMATION BUT A DEMONSTRATION

God is a God of miracles.

Remove the miraculous from the Old and New Testament and you have very little left. The Old Testament is packed with the miraculous. Angelic visitations, a woman of ninety and her ninety-nine-year-old husband having a child, a burning bush, parted seas, manna from heaven, water from a rock, the sick being healed, the dead being raised to life again, prophetic messages and dramatic deliverances are just a few of the miracles in God's Word. Even the Law and the dimensions of measurements for the tabernacle were given supernaturally!

In preparing the Bible study in the Book of Acts for the Appendix of this book, I began by listing the verses that referred to the miraculous. I soon realised that it was far easier to list the verses that didn't refer to the miraculous! There was a flow of healings, prophecies, visions, angelic visitations and miraculous deliverances from prison. It was a fascinating study (see Appendix 3). I also believe that the Book of Acts is not just a history book but a pattern and design for the Church.

The gospel accounts of the life of Jesus are packed with the miraculous. Even such events as the Sermon on the Mount and the feeding of the five thousand followed Jesus' healing ministry.

Have you ever wondered why such large crowds were there? Did you think it was just because of Jesus' preaching? Then read the Scriptures again.

> *Now Jesus went about all Galilee, teaching in their synagogues, preaching the gospel of the kingdom, and healing all kinds of sickness and all kinds of disease among the people. Then His fame went throughout all Syria; and they brought to Him all sick people who were afflicted with various diseases and torments and those who were demon-possessed, epileptics, and paralytics; and He healed them.* Great multitudes followed Him – from Galilee, and from Decapolis, Jerusalem, Judea, and beyond the Jordan. And seeing the multitudes, He went up on a mountain, and when He was seated His disciples came to Him. Then He opened His mouth and taught them, saying: 'Blessed are the poor in spirit, for theirs is the kingdom of heaven. Blessed are those who mourn, for they shall be comforted. Blessed are the meek, for they shall inherit the earth.' Matthew 4:23 – 5:5

> And He came down with them and stood on a level place with a crowd of His disciples and *a great multitude* of people from all Judea and Jerusalem, and from the sea-coast of Tyre and Sidon, who *came to hear Him and be healed of their diseases, as well as those who were tormented with unclean spirits. And they were healed. And the whole multitude sought to touch Him, for power went out from Him and healed them all. Then He lifted up His eyes toward His disciples, and said:* 'Blessed are you poor, for yours is the kingdom of God!' Luke 6:17–20

Until I saw these verses, I always used to wonder how such large crowds gathered.

The Bible's account of what is commonly called the feeding of the 5,000, again tells us why they were there: 'A great multitude followed Him because they saw His signs which He performed on those who were diseased.' (See John 6:2–5)

> And the apostles, when they had returned, told Him all that they had done. And He took them and went aside privately into a deserted place belonging to the city called Bethsaida. *But when the multitudes knew it, they followed Him; and He received them and spoke to them*

> *about the kingdom of God, and healed those who had need of healing.* When the day began to wear away, the twelve came and said to Him, 'Send the multitude away, that they may go into the surrounding towns and country, and lodge and get provisions; for we are in a deserted place here.' But He said to them, 'You give them something to eat.' And they said, 'We have no more than five loaves and two fish, unless we go and buy food for all these people.' For there were about five thousand men. And He said to His disciples, 'Make them sit down in groups of fifty.' And they did so, and made them all sit down. Then He took the five loaves and the two fish, and looking up to heaven, He blessed and broke them, and gave them to the disciples to set before the multitude. So they all ate and were filled, and twelve baskets of the leftover fragments were taken up by them. Luke 9:10–17

> When Jesus heard it, He departed from there by boat to a deserted place by Himself. But when the multitudes heard it, they followed Him on foot from the cities. *And when Jesus went out He saw a great multitude; and He was moved with compassion for them, and healed their sick.* When it was evening, His disciples came to Him, saying, 'This is a deserted place, and the hour is already late. Send the multitudes away, that they may go into the villages and buy themselves food.' But Jesus said to them, 'They do not need to go away. You give them something to eat.' Matthew 14:13–16

Christianity without the supernatural is like Samson without hair, powerless to deliver this generation.

Paul said, 'My speech and my preaching were not with persuasive words of human wisdom, but in *demonstration of the Spirit and of power,* that your faith should not rest in the wisdom of men, but in the power of God' (1 Corinthians 2:4,5). How many today could honestly say these words summed up their own ministry?

A recent research project concluded that of the 87,000 pages of theological reference works in the library of a prominent evangelical seminary, only 288 touched on God's power. That is about one third of one per cent. No wonder many of our theological colleges have produced generations of relatively powerless ministers. Yet, Jesus came both, '*preaching* and *showing* the glad tidings of the Kingdom of God' (Luke 8:1).

The gospel of the Kingdom can be both seen and heard.

It is worth noting the pattern of Jesus' ministry wherever he went:

1. PROCLAMATION: He preached repentance and the good news of the Kingdom of God

2. DEMONSTRATION: He healed the sick, raised the dead and cast out demons.

So often, all we have offered is lots of words and little action.

When John the Baptist was having doubts as to whether Jesus was the Messiah and sent some of his disciples to check up, saying, 'Are You the coming one or do we look for another?' Jesus did not say, 'Take him a copy of my sermon notes, that will convince him.' Rather, he **demonstrated** who He was.

> That very hour He cured many people of their infirmities, afflictions and evil spirits: and to many who were blind He gave sight. Luke 7:21

Then He told those sent to Him, 'Go and tell John the things you have **seen** and **heard**: that the blind see, the lame walk, the lepers are cleansed, the deaf hear, the dead are raised, the poor have the gospel preached to them' (Matthew 11:2–6; Luke 7:19–22).

> Jesus Christ is the same, yesterday, today and forever. Hebrews 13:8

As in the days when Christ walked this earth, miracles are still a key to evangelism today.

Note that although 1 Corinthians 12 differentiates between the gifts of healings and miracles, I have in this section used the term 'miracle' in its wider context to include healing. for I believe that any answer to prayer is a miracle.

10 MIRACLES ARE A KEY TO EVANGELISM

I had been a Christian for thirty-eight years and in professional Christian work as a missionary and a seminary professor for twenty-six of those years. But I had never seen anything like this! It soon became obvious that I had been missing an important dimension of Christianity for all those years.

Charles H. Kraft
Professor of Anthropology & Inter-cultural Communication
Fuller Theological Seminary, Pasadena, California
Christianity with Power, Servant Books © 1989
(Used with permission.)

The above extract was written after witnessing healings.

The preaching of the gospel with signs following always caused great multitudes to gather and to believe. (See Matthew 4:23–25; Matthew 15:30,31; Mark 1:32–34; Luke 5:15.)

> A great multitude followed Him, because they *saw* His signs which He performed on those who were diseased. John 6:2

> Many believed in His Name when they *saw* the signs which He did. John 2:23

When Philip went down to Samaria and preached Christ 'the multitudes with one accord heeded the things spoken by

Philip, **hearing and seeing** the miracles which he did' (Acts 8:6).

We read of whole cities turning to the Lord when they saw the gospel proclaimed with signs following.

How we need to see such a demonstration of God's power on our streets today! I believe that visual testimonies of neighbours miraculously healed, will still lead many to turn to Christ today.

Peter 'went down to the saints who dwelt in Lydda. There he found a certain man named Aeneas, who had been bedridden eight years and was paralysed. And he spoke the word, "Aeneas, Jesus Christ heals you. Arise and make your bed". Then he arose immediately. So all who dwelt at Lydda and Sharon saw him and turned to the Lord' (Acts 9:32–35).

Nine times in the Book of Acts signs and wonders, along with preaching, were the keys to Church growth. On another eight occasions Church growth was the direct result of signs and wonders. **Rarely was Church growth attributed to preaching alone** (see Appendix 2). In Japan, I walked through the streets of Tokyo and past the shrines packed with people praying to golden Buddhas. Yet the people never experience answered prayer.

I stood and watched as the sick flocked to the brass idols to pray for healing. How I longed to share with all of them that we have a God who hears and can answer prayer. Only the gospel preached with signs following will reach a people so entrenched in religion and ancestral worship.

Everyone has needs. Everyone has loved ones who are sick and suffering. There is one language understood by all – the language of miracles.

In Hong Kong I saw the people kneeling before the golden Buddhas. They clapped their hands loudly and banged pieces of wood together, hoping to catch Buddha's attention. But Buddha just sat there with his arms folded and his eyes closed.

But our God's eyes are not closed and His arms are not folded. His hand is outstretched to save and to heal.

I have found that Africans and Asians are very aware of the spirit world. So, when western missionaries have come without the miraculous message of Christ, the people have generally not been impressed. Sadly, there has seemed to be more visible power in their old ways than in Christianity.

The Interdenominational and Foreign Mission Association (IFMA) and the Evangelical Foreign Missions Association (EFMA) recently held a joint study conference at the US Centre For World Mission in Pasadena, California. Ron Blue, Professor of Missions at Dallas Theological Seminary, in his opening address reported that one of the chief problems among the believers in the churches planted by evangelical missions in Africa is the 'frighteningly large number of Christian believers who still rely on the witch-doctor whenever a serious problem comes into their lives.' We are not just talking about new converts either, but Sunday school teachers, elders and even pastors.

How can this be?

I believe that one of the major problems is that our Western Bible Colleges have so often sent out missionaries who were not equipped in God's Word concerning the Lord's power to heal and deliver, so the African people went back to the witch-doctors who had deceived their tribes for generations with demonic signs and wonders. Their old gods made it rain, gave them victories in battle and cursed their enemies. The white man's God seemed powerless. **How terrible this is when we have an Almighty God!**

Some Africans believed, but there was often a dual allegiance, where they attended church on Sunday, but went to the witch-doctor when they were sick, in trouble or experiencing family problems. This led to many converts falling away. On Sunday they heard about this wonderful healer called Jesus. They were told that He had risen from the dead and was alive today. They were called to pledge allegiance to Him and then told that He no longer worked miracles.

One native woman, when asked by a missionary why she went to the witch-doctor when her child was sick, pointed to the beautiful church across the way and replied, 'White man, he would say a short prayer for God to bless my child, to teach me something through the sickness and ask for His will to be done. That is all. And nothing would happen.'

Another added, 'But white man does not believe in his God like we believe in our Ju Ju gods.'

Yet time and time again I have seen these pagan gods abandoned, broken into pieces and burned on bonfires, when the people see evidence of the living, resurrected Christ in their midst. People are no different today than in Jesus' day, when 'a great multitude followed Him, because they saw His miracles which He did on them that were diseased.'

David Wang, General Director of Asian Outreach says that one of the most significant factors stimulating the growth of Christianity in China to more than 30 million in 1982 was a widespread, spontaneous outbreak of supernatural signs and wonders in every province.

Most of the people in America, Canada, Australia, New Zealand and Europe believe that Jesus once lived, but is now dead and therefore has no real relevance to them today. They say, 'If Jesus is alive, why doesn't he do the same things he did 2,000 years ago?' How we need to see a new demonstration of the kingdom in our streets, cities, towns and villages.

Over recent years there has been a growing emphasis on 'power evangelism', for which I rejoice. But we must never isolate 'signs and wonders' from evangelism. God's power to heal the sick, cast out demons and perform miracles is not an end in itself. The end result must be that God is glorified and men and women are reconciled to Him. 'Signs' do not point at themselves but to something or someone else. Miracles are not an end in themselves but point us to Jesus and the reliability of God's Word.

Tommy Lee Osborn and his young wife, Daisy, had both received Christ in their early teens and longed to serve Him, so, they went to India as missionaries and sought to share the message of Christ with the people. They used the Scriptures to show the Hindu and Muslim inhabitants that Jesus Christ was the Son of God, but failed to make one convert. They tried to convince the Muslims about Jesus Christ by showing them scripture verses, but the Muslims just showed the Osborns the Koran, which to them, was God's word given by the mouth of their prophet Mohammed.

So, having studied the language, preached, entertained visitors and spent long hours in theological discourses without one person coming to Christ, the Osborns returned home feeling complete failures. On arriving back in America they shut themselves away for months on end, earnestly searching the Scriptures for an answer to their dilemma and their fruitlessness in ministry.

A major breakthrough came when Daisy said, 'Let's read the New Testament as though we had never read it in our lives, like it was a new book.' She later testified, 'As we read the New Testament, I will never forget the shock as we discovered scripture after scripture where Jesus gave us authority over demons and over disease, to speak in His Name.'

Attending a massive healing crusade, where many were healed, sealed their new conviction that preaching the gospel with signs following was the key to mass evangelism. Daisy said, 'It was the first time in my life I had ever seen miracles, even though I had accepted Jesus at the age of twelve. I was a grown woman, a wife, a mother, and had been a missionary in India, yet I had never seen an instant miracle.'

T. L. added, 'We had faithfully prayed for the sick wherever we ministered. But it was almost a ritual. Every Friday night in our meetings, we prayed for the sick. We didn't see much happen, but we prayed.'

They decided to make announcements in the newspapers and on the radio inviting people to bring those who were sick and declaring that God would heal them. Night after night they preached and then they prayed together for any who were sick. One after another was miraculously healed.

Despite their new found effectiveness in ministry, they knew that they still had a call to go to the unreached peoples of the world. With no funds to return to India, they set out for the nearby Caribbean island of Jamaica. For thirteen weeks they preached and prayed for the sick seeing over 9,000 people come forward and kneel to pray the sinner's prayer, accepting Christ. Hundreds more testified to receiving healing. As Daisy put it, 'We saw more fruit from our labours in a single night than we had seen in the previous seven years. **It was miracles that made the difference.**'

From Jamaica, they went on to Puerto Rico, Cuba, Central and South America, Japan, Thailand and Java. Everywhere the multitudes gathered and seeing the miracles, thousands turned to Christ.

Now they felt it was time to return to India. They went back to the same city and there on a big open field by the great stadium in the University City of Lucknow they set up their platform.

Several notable miracles took place and soon over 60,000 people gathered!

As Daisy later said, 'The people had not changed. The situation had not changed. But we had changed. Our thinking had been changed. Our lives had been changed. We knew God would fulfil His Word.'

Seeing the miracles, Hindus and Muslims in their thousands began to turn to the Lord.

One evening during a crusade in Java, a Muslim priest started up the platform steps to interrupt T. L. Osborn, while he was preaching.

The priest said, 'That man is false. Jesus is dead. He's not God's Son. Let me speak to the people about Mohammed, God's true prophet.' Daisy tried to reason with him but he was angry. He really felt he had a right to speak.

Finally she told him: 'Listen, here's what I'll do: I'll interrupt my husband on one condition. You and I will go together to the microphone. We will not argue. We will **show** which prophet is true and alive. We'll call for someone totally blind to come forward. You pray for him in the presence of the people, in the name of Mohammed, and if he sees, we'll believe on your prophet. Then I'll pray for him in the Name of Jesus, and if he sees, then all of your people will know that what the Bible says about Christ is true, that He is God's Son and that God has raised Him from the dead.'

The young Muslim priest refused, turned in a fit of anger and strode away.

Since that time T. L. and Daisy have travelled to over seventy nations of the world holding crusades. Everywhere they have gone, the same thing has happened; tens of thousands of Muslims, Hindus, Sikhs, Buddhists and agnostics gather, most never having heard the message of Christ before. Yet, when the gospel is proclaimed in power and confirmed with signs following, the people turn to Christ by the thousands. Missionaries have recorded whole communities turning to the Lord during their crusades.

Miracles are a key to evangelism!

Professor Peter Wagner is highly regarded for his research into the subject of Church growth, especially in Latin America. His background is that of a Scofield Bible Dispensational Evangelical, in other words, believing that signs and wonders are not for today and that miracles have ceased. Therefore, his discoveries surprised him. He concluded, 'What I am seeing, as the picture is beginning to emerge, is that world-wide there is a remarkably close relationship between growth of the churches today and the healing ministry – particularly but not exclusively in areas where the gospel has just penetrated.' (See *A Third Wave* by C. Peter Wagner.)

Wagner added, 'Much to my surprise, I began to discover that the churches that were far outweighing all the others were the Pentecostal churches.'

I do not share this to promote a denomination (I am a Baptist minister) but rather to emphasise the importance of an openness to the Holy Spirit's power today.

Wagner concluded, 'Across the board, the most effective evangelism in today's world is accompanied by manifestations of supernatural power. Nine out of ten of the world's largest churches are Pentecostal or Charismatic and there are now over 240 million Pentecostal and Charismatic Christians in the world today.'

Charles Kraft, Professor of Anthropology and Intercultural Communications at Fuller Theological Seminary, Pasadena, California, commented after he had seen God heal the sick: 'I had been a Christian for thirty-eight years and in professional Christian work as a missionary and a seminary professor for twenty-six of those years. But I had never seen anything like this! It soon became obvious that I had been missing an important dimension of Christianity for all those years.'

God is opening our eyes afresh to the power available to the church in Jesus' Name.

Listen to Jesus' words when confronted by the religious sceptic of His day:

> The Jewish leaders surrounded him and asked Him, 'If you are the Christ tell us plainly.' Jesus replied: 'The proof is in the miracles I do in the name of My Father ... do not believe Me unless I do the miracles of God. And if I do, then believe them even if you do not believe in Me. The proof is in the miracles I do in My Father's Name.' John 10:24,25,37 TLB

Times have not changed. As in Bible days, multitudes follow Jesus when they see His miracles (John 6:2).

> Now there was a man of the Pharisees, named Nicodemus, a ruler of the Jews; this man came to Him by night, and said to Him, 'Rabbi, we know that You have come from God as a teacher; for no one can do these signs that you do unless God is with him.' John 3:1,2

Nicodemus believed that Jesus had come from God, not because of the words that Jesus spoke, as wonderful as they were, but because of the signs (miracles) that He did. Not only Nicodemus, but the disciples themselves believed in Jesus because of His signs:

> This beginning of His signs Jesus did in Cana of Galilee, and manifested His glory, and His disciples believed in Him. John 2:11

After turning water into wine at Cana, Jesus went to Jerusalem for the Passover. This is what happened there:

> Now when He was in Jerusalem at the Passover, during the feast, many believed in His Name, beholding His signs which He was doing. John 2:23

It was on seeing Lazarus raised from the dead that many of the Jews believed in Jesus:

> The great multitude therefore of the Jews learned that He was there; and they came, not for Jesus' sake only, but that they might also see Lazarus, whom He raised from the dead. But the chief priests took counsel that they might put Lazarus to death also; because on account of him many of the Jews were going away, and were believing in Jesus. John 12:9–11

They believed that Jesus' words were words from God, not because of His persuasiveness or His logical arguments, but because of the signs, wonders and miracles that He did. It was in this manner that Jesus preached the gospel, not only in words, but in demonstration of the power of God. If we are to be like Jesus, we must spread the gospel in the same way too.

Miracles are a key to evangelism.

11 MIRACLES DEMONSTRATE THAT JESUS IS ALIVE

I was amazed at the contrast between the traditional methods of evangelisation and this. The Bible method of mighty miracle ministry results in an amazing harvest of souls. I witnessed thousands willingly accept the Lord Jesus Christ as their personal saviour.

One night I witnessed eight totally blind people instantly healed. I ask myself as a missionary: who would ever go back to the old traditional methods which, for years, have proved to be ineffective in winning the masses, when we now see the New Testament method producing such glorious results?

As a missionary, who has laboured among non-Christians for many years, I am convinced that miracle evangelism is the only means of reaching the masses today and of convincing them that Jesus Christ is alive, the same yesterday and today and forever.

Rev Harold Groves
Modern Miracles in Mombasa, an OSFO Publication
(Used with permission.)

The above was written after witnessing the miracles at T. L. and Daisy Osborn's Mombasa Crusade. Rev Groves had, prior to this, served the Lord for sixteen years in India with very few results.

'Why should they believe me when I tell them that Jesus is the only way to God and to forsake their other gods?'

The thought passed through my mind as I came to the conclusion of my message to the crowd that had gathered, on the first night of one of my African crusades. Many of them were in Muslim robes and stood looking on sceptically.

The Holy Spirit reminded me that it is because Jesus truly is the Son of God and alive today.

'Mohammed is dead, but Jesus is alive!' I proclaimed. 'But don't just take my word for it. He is going to prove it by healing the sick.'

I paused. 'I want every blind person to come forward.' Several in the crowd began to move, bringing blind folk forward. Suddenly, everyone stopped as they saw someone bringing to the front the local blind beggar, who had not been in the meeting thus far, but had been walking past.

The Lord seemed to fill my heart with faith at that point. 'In Jesus' Name, be healed and receive your sight.' Immediately he began to jump and shout excitedly, 'I can see! I can see!' Then he began to describe the beautiful surroundings he had never seen before.

The crowd went wild. I asked how many knew this man and knew that he was blind; almost every hand was raised. The people eagerly turned to the Lord.

After this, other blind were brought forward along with many who were deaf. At the end of the crusade, the local ministers and missionaries went among the people and reported that they could not find anyone who had been prayed for and not healed.

Signs and wonders demonstrate that we do not serve a dead God, but that Jesus is alive today! Most people acknowledge that Christ once lived, but believe that He is now dead. Yet when they see the miracles, they know that He is alive. The Muslims believe that Jesus once lived, they believe that He was a prophet and that He healed the sick. However, they believe that He is now dead.

There is only one argument to win a Muslim. If Jesus is alive, let Him do the miracles which He did before. If He is dead, He cannot. Time and again during my overseas crusades I have seen Muslims turn to Christ in their thousands when they have seen the miracles. When they see Jesus healing the sick, Muslims will freely exchange their dead prophet for a living Saviour.

Today, as in Bible days, many have 'believed when they saw His miracles which He did on them that were diseased (John 6:2). Today, just as in Bible days, Jesus is willing to 'show Himself alive by many infallible proofs' (Acts 1:3).

12 MIRACLES CONFIRM GOD'S WORD

'These signs *will* follow those who believe: In my name they will cast out demons; they will speak with new tongues; they will take up serpents; and if they drink anything deadly, it will by no means hurt them: they will lay hands on the sick and they will recover.' So then, after the Lord had spoken to them, He was received up into heaven and sat down at the right hand of God. And they went out and preached everywhere, the Lord working *with them* confirming the word through the accompanying signs. Amen. Mark 16:17–20

Notice that we are not just called to work **for** God but to work **with** Him. Paul pointed out to the Corinthian Church that we are 'workers together with Him' (2 Corinthians 6:1) and 'God's fellow workers' (1 Corinthians 3:9).

What a great thrill and privilege in ministry, just to cooperate with the Lord.

As the disciples went out, the Lord **bore witness** to what they said, as He had promised, 'both with signs and wonders, with various miracles and gifts of the Holy Spirit' (Hebrews 2:4).

> They stayed there [Iconium] a long time, speaking boldly in the Lord, who was *bearing witness* to the word of His grace, granting signs and wonders to be done by their hands. Acts 14:3

When God confirms His Word with signs following everyone knows who is speaking.

> 'Men of Israel, hear these words; Jesus of Nazareth, a man *attested by God* to you by miracles, wonders and signs which God did through Him in your midst.' Acts 2:22

> The multitudes with one accord heeded the things spoken by Philip, hearing and seeing the miracles which he did. Acts 8:6

God 'confirmed the Word through the accompanying signs.' In other words, God said, 'Amen, I agree with what you've preached,' and confirmed it with miracles.

When I preach the gospel, especially among those who have never heard the message of Christ before, I expect God to 'confirm' His Word with signs following. Most of the unreached peoples of our world are religious. Turning to Christ may well bring persecution. They need to see a demonstration of the truth of the gospel in its fullness.

When I preach in Muslim lands, I hold up my Bible and say that Jesus is the only way to God. Some of the Muslims then get their black book and say, 'No, He is not.' I hold up my Bible and say, 'This is God's Word.' They may hold up their copies of the Koran and say, 'No, this is.'

Who is right? Both are holding black leather bound books with gold lettering.

I say, 'Let the true God answer by fire!' (It is not original, I got the idea from Elijah). The God of Elijah is just as powerful today!

When I preach that Jesus is the Son of God, that He died for our sins and rose again, I stand on the promises of God's Word, that He will confirm His Word with signs following.

It is God's, 'Amen, I agree.'

On seeing the miracles, we have seen Muslims turn to Christ in their thousands. What a joy to see those who have passively accepted every sickness and adverse circumstance as 'the will of Allah', healed in Jesus' Name and discover that it is not God's will for them.

When the Pharisees questioned Jesus' identity saying, 'Why does this man speak blasphemies like this? Who can forgive sins but God alone?' (Mark 2:7), Jesus replied:

> '*That you may know* that the Son of Man has power on earth to forgive sin,' (He said to the paralytic,) 'I say to you, arise, take up your bed, and go to your house.' Immediately he arose, took up the bed and went out in the presence of them all, so that all were amazed and gloried God, saying, 'We never saw anything like this.'
> Mark 2:10–12

Jesus said, 'That you may know.' He proved who He was and the truth of His words, by healing the paralytic.

Today, many still doubt Jesus' true identity and miracles attest to our message.

13 MIRACLES DEMONSTRATE CHRIST'S TOTAL VICTORY OVER SATAN

We need to see that Satan is a squatter!

The Collins Concise Dictionary describes 'to squat' as, 'to occupy land to which the occupant has no legal title' and 'a squatter' as 'a person who occupies land wrongfully.' Squatters move into someone else's property and take up residence, refusing to leave. Although they have no legal right to be there, an eviction order is required to get them out.

This is God's world and He has given us an eviction order for Satan, drawn up in the courts of heaven (see Psalms 24:1; 47:7). Jesus has 'all authority' (Matthew 28:18) and has delegated that authority to us, to act on His behalf. He has given us power and authority over demons and to heal the sick (see also Luke 9:1,2, Matthew 10:1). Every sickness healed and every demon cast out is territory taken for the Lord Jesus. No wonder Satan wants to stop the Church recognising its authority in Christ! Satan's kingdom is collapsing.

We often speak of 'praying for healing', but you could not label how Jesus ministered to the sick as 'praying'. He just spoke the Word:

'Be made whole'
'Receive your sight'
'Stretch out your hand'
'Lazarus, come forth'
'Deaf ears, be opened'
'I am willing – be cleansed'

'Take up your bed and walk'

The early Church followed His example:

'In the Name of Jesus Christ of Nazareth, rise up and walk'
'Tabitha, arise'
'Aeneas, Jesus the Christ heals you, arise and make your bed'

When we recognise the source of sickness and our authority in Jesus' Name, we too can speak with the same boldness.

So much 'prayer for the sick' is done in unbelief, with no expectation for a recovery. It is significant that there are no biblical accounts of Christ praying for the sick. He usually just spoke healing to the person; 'Be made whole,' or, 'Rise, take up your bed and walk.' He commanded the condition to be made well (Luke 4:39; 5:13; 7:6–10) or the spirit to leave (Luke 4:35) or the person being healed to do something in faith (Luke 5:24; 6:10; 7:14). Sometimes He would touch the person (Luke 5:13). At other times people would touch Him and be healed (Luke 8:44, Matthew 14:36). It seems that He did His praying before His deeds, not during them.

I don't believe that 'pray' is the main word for what we are called to do. I believe that we are called to take authority over demons and sickness just as Jesus did. Jesus said, 'He who believes in me, the works that I do, he will do also, and greater works than these he will do' (John 14:12).

Our Lord simply, 'sent forth his word and healed them.'

> When evening had come, they brought to him many who were demon-possessed. And He cast out the spirits *with a word* and healed all who were sick. Matthew 8:16

We have so often failed to realise the power in the word spoken by faith in the Name of Jesus (see also John 4:46–54; Luke 17:11–19). The centurion realised this when he said to Jesus, 'Only speak the word and my servant will be healed' (Matthew 8:8). He got what he believed for!

The same Jesus who called disciples together, 'gave them power and authority over all demons, and to cure diseases' and 'sent them to preach the Kingdom of God, and to heal the sick' (Luke 9:1,2), has said of all those who believe, 'In my name they will cast out demons. They will lay hands on the sick and they will recover' (Mark 16:17,18).

This is the Ph.D. that we need if we are to be effective for the Kingdom – preaching, healing and deliverance!

When we go in Jesus' Name we go on His behalf. I go with His authority and declare:

> 'Sickness, go in the Name of Jesus!'
> 'Demons, out in the Name of Jesus!'

The battle was won at Calvary and now we go in Christ's victory and with His authority. I believe that God is raising up an army of believers in this day to go in His power and to see territory taken from Satan and restored to its rightful owner, King Jesus. The same Jesus who healed the sick and set captives free, has now said to the believer, 'I give *you* power over unclean spirits to cast them out and to heal all kinds of sickness and all kinds of diseases' (Matthew 10:1).

For years ministers have prayed, 'Lord, heal this person, if it be Thy will.' Yet Jesus has already told us, 'Whatever city you enter and they receive you, eat such things as are set before you. And heal the sick who are there, and say to them, "The Kingdom of God has come near to you" ' (Luke 10:8,9). Healing the sick is as much a scriptural command as baptising disciples.

So often we play 'unspiritual tennis' with God. When God gives us a job to do, we so often just knock the ball back into His court. He says, 'I have given you authority to do this,' and we pray, 'Lord, you do it.' The Lord says, 'Lay hands on the sick and they will recover,' yet we pray from a distance, 'Lord, lay your healing hand on that sick person.' The Lord says of believers, 'They will cast out demons in My Name,' and we pray, 'Lord, that person needs setting free; set them free Lord.' We pray, 'Lord, that brother really needs You to train him and shape his life.' Jesus said, 'Go and make disciples.' We pray, 'Lord, care for these new Christians.' Jesus says, 'Shepherd My sheep.'

So often we are like Gideon, who prayed, 'O my Lord, if the Lord is with us, why then has all this happened to us and where are all His miracles which our fathers told us about, saying, "did not the Lord bring us up from Egypt?" But now the Lord has forsaken us and delivered us into the hand of the Midianites' (Judges 6:13).

It was true that God did lead His people out of Egypt; however Moses was His instrument. God parted the Red Sea, but if Moses had not held his rod over the waters, they would have stayed closed, because this was the way God had chosen for the miracle to take place. It is true that God caused water to come from the rock, but only when Moses hit it.

The Lord's reply to Gideon was somewhat of a surprise: 'Go in this your strength and deliver Israel from the hand of Midian. Have I not sent you?' (Judges 6:14).

God was saying, 'Yes, I can deliver your nation from the hand of Midian, but I will use you as my instrument to do it.' The Lord has not called His saints just to be spectators, but to be actively involved in the things He is doing.

On the cross, Jesus won a total victory over Satan. However, we do not see the full manifestation of that victory yet. The situations we find ourselves in have been compared to World War II. On 'D-Day' the Allied troops established their beach-head in Normandy. The war in Europe was really won. Yet 'V-E Day', Victory Day, still stood ahead. The battles still went on, though ultimate victory was secured. On the cross Jesus' victory over Satan was established. Yet we still await 'V-E Day' at Christ's return.

This may help us to understand the victory which is ours in Christ, yet the fact that we are daily involved in spiritual warfare.

Between 'D-Day' and 'V-E Day' mopping-up campaigns were needed to possess enemy-held territory. The same is true for the soldier of Christ. We can see enemy-held territory re-possessed in Jesus' Name. The battle is as real as it was in the days of the early Church (Satan is not a dispensationalist).

Yet the same Holy Spirit power and the same authority in the Name of Jesus is ours today.

'For this purpose the Son of God was manifested, that he might destroy the works of the devil' (1 John 3:8). The Greek word used here for 'destroy' *(luo)* basically means 'to become unglued, to loose or cause to lose consistence'. An example of this would be when the mortar of a building is rotten so that it begins crumbling and disintegrating. Everything Satan has built is breaking down! Each person who follows Jesus, each one healed and set free, is territory taken from Satan's crumbling kingdom.

Where are the Elijahs today who dare to stand up and say, 'If the Lord is God, follow Him, but if Baal then follow him...The God who answers by fire, He is God'? (1 Kings 18:25–39). Where are the men and women of God who will show up the false prophets around us for what they are?

14 MIRACLES DEMONSTRATE THAT GOD CARES

The fact that many wonderful miracle healings are occurring today in great public healing rallies, who can deny? Only those deny who have not been and seen. With my own eyes almost jumping out of their sockets, I have seen the dumb from birth given speech, the stone deaf given new hearing, the long blind suddenly given new vision, terminal cancer instantaneously cured (and later medically attested), crippled arthritics released and straightened on the spot, wheelchair victims of multiple sclerosis wheel their own chairs away, not to mention other such wonderful healings.

Dr J. Sidlow Baxter, Bible Teacher
Divine Healing of the Body, Zondervan
Publication © 1979
(Used with permission.)

Then a leper came to Him, imploring Him, kneeling down to Him and saying to Him, 'If you are willing, you can make me clean.' Jesus moved with compassion, put out His hand and touched Him and said to Him, 'I am willing, be cleansed.' As soon as He had spoken, immediately the leprosy left him and he was cleansed. Mark 1:40–42

When Jesus went out He saw a great multitude; and He was moved with compassion for them and healed their sick. Matthew 14:14

> Now as they went out of Jericho, a great multitude followed Him. And behold, two blind men sitting by the road, when they heard that Jesus was passing by, cried out, saying, 'Have mercy on us, O Lord, Son of David!' Then the multitude warned them that they should be quiet; but they cried out all the more, saying, 'Have mercy on us, O Lord, Son of David!' So Jesus stood still and called them, and said, 'What do you want Me to do for you?' They said to Him, 'Lord, that our eyes may be opened.' So Jesus had compassion and touched their eyes. And immediately their eyes received sight, and they followed Him. Matthew 20:29–34

In his book *Holy Spirit Baptism*, A. A. Hoekema wrote in reference to miracles: 'Their function was to authenticate the gospel when it was first preached.' His conclusion was that they are therefore no longer needed. Many other Christians have taken this stand too and preached that signs and wonders were merely to demonstrate God's power to 'get the church started', but passed away with the early Church leaders or on completion of the Canon of Scripture.

However, if that were so, how do we account for the tens of thousands of believers around the world who claim to have been healed over recent years?

Accounts of miracles can be found throughout church history, except for periods of great apostasy. Even today, unbelief will still rob us of the miraculous.

IRENAEUS (AD 140–203) in *Against Heresies Book 2* (chapter 32) wrote, 'Those who are in truth His disciples, receiving grace from Him, do in His name perform miracles, so as to promote the welfare of other men, according to the gift which each one has received from Him. For some do certainly and truly drive out devils, so that those who have thus been cleansed from evil spirits frequently both believe [in Christ], and join themselves to the Church. Others have foreknowledge of things to come; they see visions, and utter prophetic expressions. Others still heal the sick by laying their hands upon them, and they are made whole. Yea, moreover, as I have said, the dead even have been raised up and remained among us for many years.'

JUSTIN MARTYR (AD 165) wrote, 'For numberless demoniacs throughout the whole world and in your city, many of our Christian men, exorcising them in the Name of Jesus Christ, who was crucified under Pontius Pilate, have healed and do heal, rendering helpless and driving the possessing devils out of the men, though they could not be cured by all the other exorcists, and those who used incantations and drugs' (Apol. 11, chapter 6).

AMBROSE (AD 339–397) stated in *The Holy Spirit*, that healings and tongues were still given by God.

AUGUSTINE (AD 354–430), who initially thought that the first century gifts of the Spirit had died out, later in his ministry prayed for the sick, saw healings and cast out demons. In *The City of God Book 22* (chapter 28), he wrote, 'It is sometimes objected that the miracles, which Christians claimed to have occurred, no longer happen. The truth is that even today miracles are being wrought in the name of Christ.' He later gave cases of a blind man whose sight was restored, a woman healed of cancer, a doctor healed of gout, a man healed of paralysis and a friend's son raised from the dead in Jesus' Name. He concluded that there were too many miracles to list them all (Deferrari 24:433–445).

God never intended miracles to cease. But soon apostasy began to replace simple faith in Jesus Christ. It was not miracles that began to 'pass away' around the fourth century AD, but simple faith in God's Word.

Jesus said these signs will follow 'them that believe'. If you believe they will, they will. If you do not believe, then they will not.

Yet, throughout church history, there have been believers who took God's Word literally and have continued to see miracles.

THE WALDENSIANS were an evangelical community in the Middle Ages who believed James 5:14,15, that anointing the sick would bring healing and saw miracles performed in Jesus' Name.

MARTIN LUTHER (1483–1526), who had denied that the gift of healing was for his day, saw his friend Melanchthon brought back from the point of death in answer to prayer. He later encouraged prayer and the laying-on of hands for the sick, quoting Jesus' words from Mark 16: 'These signs shall follow them that believe; they shall lay hands on the sick and they shall recover.' He quoted cases of answered prayer for healing on behalf of others in his *Letters of Spiritual Counsel*. Luther wrote, 'How often it has happened, and still does, that devils have been driven out in the name of Christ; also, by calling on His Name and prayer, that the sick have been healed.'

When asked what to do for a man who was mentally ill, Luther wrote instructions for a healing service based on the New Testament letter of James, adding, 'This is what we do, and what we have been accustomed to do, for a cabinet-maker here was similarly afflicted with madness and we cured him by prayer in Christ's Name.'

Like Augustine before him, Luther came to value this precious ministry that he had once doubted and denied.

Listen to the famous **COUNT ZINZENDORF**'s words, spoken in 1730: 'To believe against hope is the root of the gift of miracles; and I owe this testimony to our beloved church, that Apostolic powers are there manifested. We have had undeniable proofs thereof in the unequivocal discovery of things, persons, and circumstances, which could not humanly have been discovered, in the healing of maladies in themselves incurable, such as cancers, consumptions, when the patient was in the agonies of death, all by means of prayer, or of a single word' (Rev A. Bost, *History of United Brethren*).

JOHN WESLEY wrote in his Journals, 'The grand reason why the miraculous gifts were so soon withdrawn, was not only that faith and holiness were well nigh lost, but that dry, formal, orthodox men began even then to ridicule whatever gifts they had not themselves; and to decry them all as either madness or imposture.'

Throughout the history of the Church, despite periods of apostasy, there was usually a remnant of believers who continued to expect and to see the miraculous.

To put a question mark over the possibility of miracles today, throws doubt on the ministry and integrity of such men of God as Martin Luther and John Wesley. Wesley recorded over 200 supernatural miracles in his Journals.

If the age of miracles has passed, Wesley, Finney and Whitefield, men used by God in the great revivals of bygone days, who all claimed to see miracles, must have been liars.

Also, the concept that miracles were only for a limited period, is based on the error that Jesus healed merely to prove His Divinity and that, now we have the Word of God, we no longer need miracles to believe.

However, the Scriptures tell us that when Jesus was tempted to use His power merely to prove who He was, He refused to do so (See Matthew 4:4–7). Although many have turned to Christ and still do so, after witnessing a demonstration of His supernatural power, Christ's main purpose in healing was because He cares! (See Matthew 20:33; Mark 5:19; 6:34; 8:2–10; Luke 17:11–17).

Do you believe that God cares for us any less today?

Could the loving Son of God, who had compassion on the sick and healed all who came in faith, cease to regard the sufferings of His own now He has been exalted to the Father's right hand?

Whatever your need is at this time, begin to reach out by faith to receive a miracle in Jesus' Name!

15 HOW TO MINISTER HEALING

The publication of this work may be regarded as a testimony of my faith in divine healing. After being stopped for more than two years in the exercise of my ministry, I was healed by the mercy of God in answer to the prayer of those who see in Him 'the Lord that healeth thee' (Exodus 15:26).

Andrew Murray, *Divine Healing*

I believe passionately in ministry to the sick!

God cares about our lost, hurting, dying world. I remember as a new Christian reading in God's Word how Jesus healed the sick nearly two thousand years ago and thinking, 'If he did it then, and He has not changed, then surely we should be seeing miracles today'. I then heard of an Anglican minister who was praying for the sick and seeing them healed. So I attended one of the meetings that he was speaking at. At the close of the service I went forward for prayer. For several years I had suffered from painful, bleeding stomach ulcers. But, before I could say anything the preacher said, 'The Lord shows me that you have stomach ulcers'. I was so shocked. This was my first encounter with the Word of Knowledge. As he laid hands on me, I was healed. From that day onwards the pain went and the bleeding stopped. I went back excitedly to my own minister and told him what the Lord had done, to which he replied, 'God does not heal the sick today.' 'Too late!' I immediately responded, 'If you had told me that last week I might have believed you, but it's too late now for God has healed me.'

More and more as I read God's Word, I saw that Jesus' ministry was not just a proclamation but also a demonstration. Not only did people receive forgiveness for their sins and the assurance of heaven when they died, but He also healed them of their sicknesses and set the captives free. I also began to see that this pattern of ministry continued through the early Church, with no indication that it should ever stop.

In this chapter let me share with you some principles that I have found to be important in ministering healing to others. I want to share general principles for ministry, rather than techniques.

One of the dangers in 'How To' books and conferences, is that people can pick up techniques from the one ministering, and miss the real key to their fruitfulness in ministry, their relationship with God. You cannot bypass an intimate walk with God and be fruitful in ministry. I knew of one minister who used to move his hand as he prayed for people. This was fine for him and the Lord used him. However, lots of the people who attended conferences that he spoke at, returned with a kind of nervous twitch when they prayed. When I asked those folks why they had suddenly started doing the same thing (as in their local church it could be off-putting and was unnecessary), they did not know. They were just copying the preacher. They had learned a technique rather than catching the spirit of the ministry.

I remember on one occasion mentioning in passing how I usually keep my eyes open as I minister, to watch to see whether the person is receiving from God. Afterwards, someone came up to me and said, 'The other week I heard another well known evangelist preach on ministering to the sick and he said that he always closes his eyes. What should I do?' I smiled and explained that we were both just sharing what worked for us. There are no hard and fast rules about such things. Each person had to come before God and discover what was right for them. We must not get side-tracked onto peripheral issues.

1. Recognise and Emphasise that Jesus is the Healer

Some time ago, I went to speak at a series of meetings. On the first night, the Lord instantly healed a man who had been deaf in one ear from birth. The word soon got around and that afternoon a woman telephoned the secretary of the church and asked, 'Is the healer going to be there again this evening?' I happened to be in the office at the time and overheard the secretary's wise answer, 'Yes, Jesus is always at our meetings.'

It reminded me of the evangelist who received a phone call asking, 'Is the healer at home?' 'Yes', the preacher replied. 'Can I speak to him?' The caller enquired. 'Just a moment,' the preacher said. Then holding the telephone in the air, he shouted, 'Jesus. There is someone on the telephone wants to speak to you.'

When I talk about healing, I am not talking about faith healing, even though faith in God for our healing is important. I have heard Christians use the term 'faith healing', but it is a term I dislike intensely. We are not 'faith healers', we are just Christians who believe that Jesus healing power is the same today! I could not heal an ant with a headache! Many people who use the term 'faith healing' claim to have healing powers of their own. I am only interested in divine healing, in Jesus the Healer. This may sound an obvious thing to say, but, I do believe that it needs emphasising strongly.

Over the years I have seen the Lord heal many thousands of people. I have had the privilege of seeing many blind receive their sight, the deaf hear, the lame walk and the dumb speak. Jesus has not changed, His power is the same today! But it was not me that healed them. If Jesus had not touched them, they would have gone home as sick as they had come to the meetings. I could never be proud of what God has done, because I know that it is not me. We are just privileged to be God's co-workers (1 Corinthians 3:9, Mark 16:20). I often say of the 'New Age' religions with their claims that we can be gods, 'Who wants to be a 'god', when we can be servants, sons and daughters and best friends with the one true and living God?'

When ministering healing, point people to Jesus. Always

exalt Jesus in your preaching. He alone is the healer. We do not minister out of our own strength or supply. There have been a few times when I have gone to minister not feeling well myself (usually because I have been overdoing it and not resting enough). But it makes no difference how I feel, for the Word of God is true and unchanging. Jesus is the same today as He was yesterday and will be the same forever (Hebrews 13:8). I remember one night, after a long and busy tour, where I had been talking at several meetings a day, croaking my way through a message on healing after nearly losing my voice. Yet God did some great miracles that night. One man had travelled over a hundred miles to be at the meeting and the Lord opened his deaf ears.

In twenty years of ministering God's Word, I can say to the glory of God that I have not missed one meeting I was supposed to be speaking at, through sickness. I did not say that I have never felt ill. The devil tries to put sickness on everyone. There have been a few occasions in Africa and Asia, where I have preached with a fever, the sweat running down my brow, propped up by a chair! But, I have never missed a meeting. There are two reasons why that is so.

Firstly, I am not going to give in and let the devil win one round! It is amusing but, usually as I preach and lift up Jesus, my own faith is released and I get healed half way through my message! Then I just kick the chair away and off I go! If I felt unwell, I would want to be in an atmosphere of faith. Some people send the amusing message to their pastor, 'I'm sorry I can't be at the healing meeting, because I am feeling sick.' In Bible days they carried people on stretchers to be where Jesus was healing the sick.

Secondly, the devil realises that, if he tries to put sickness on me, I have a goal that night to see at least ten people healed of that same problem. I will make a point of praying specifically for those with that particular need. The devil knows that he is going to lose out tenfold every time! I emphasise again that our ministering to the sick is not dependent on how we feel, because we are not doing the healing. Lift up Jesus, for He alone is the Healer.

2. Check your Motives

Why do you want God to use you? Is it for the glory of God and because you care for God's hurting world?

Although I have shared many testimonies of miracles in this book to help lift your faith, there are literally thousands of others which I have not shared. However amazing a miracle has been in one of our crusades, before I tell others, I seek first to ensure that I have gone before God alone and given Him the glory. Then, if I believe it will help others, I check with the Lord that it is alright to share it. There were a few occasions when Jesus healed people and told them to tell no-one. Although, as we have seen from God's Word, many came to Christ when they saw the miracles, we have also seen that God's primary purpose for healing people is because He cares for them.

Genuinely caring for others is an important principle in seeing God use you. Jesus was 'moved with compassion' and healed people; are we moved with compassion? Sometimes as I have travelled to meetings, tears have come into my eyes as I have looked out on the people around. They are so lost without Jesus. How I long for others to know the Lord's touch on their life. It is this burden that drives me to go to the ends of the earth with the gospel. Sometimes as I have been among a tribe living in a wooden shack, sharing my bed with hundreds of flying ants, as lizards and giant-sized cockroaches crawl around me, I have thought, 'I would rather be in the comforts of my home or sitting behind my office desk'. But a love for God and for our world should cause us to lay down our lives. Our praying will tell us how much we care about others. The amount that we give to reaching the unreached will show us how much we really care for the lost.

Ask the Lord to soften your heart and to give you something of His care for this lost world in which we live. I remember praying that prayer. As a grown man, I could not remember crying since I was four years old. But God began a process of softening my heart that day. It is so easy to get tied up in all the cares of business life, family life and even church life and to miss our main purpose for being here, to be ambassadors for Christ to our world (2 Corinthians 5:20).

Ask God to open your eyes, to see this broken world as He sees it and to feel His love for hurting, dying people.

3. See your Need of the Lord's Anointing

It is so vital that people realise that Jesus is ever present to touch and to heal. So many people say, 'If Jesus were here, I know that He would heal me.' Yet He is of course there. Our goal is to help people to see that Jesus is there with them, that they might reach out by faith to receive their healing. We do this both by pointing them to the unchanging Word of God and by the anointing of the Holy Spirit on our life and words. This is more than just speaking the right words. Anyone can say, 'Jesus is here, just believe it', but, what we need is the power of God upon our words that they might come with Divine impact. Only this can release people's faith to make them whole.

How we need the power of the Holy Spirit in our life. Jesus said,

> 'The Spirit of the Lord is upon Me, because *He has anointed Me* to preach the gospel to the poor; He has sent me to heal the broken hearted, to preach deliverance to the captives, and recovery of sight to the blind, to set at liberty them that are bruised. To preach the acceptable year of the Lord.' Luke 4:18,19

Jesus attributed the miracles and the healings that took place to the power of the Holy Spirit in His life.

In Acts 10:38 we read how, 'God anointed Jesus of Nazareth with the Holy Spirit and with power, who went about doing good and healing all who were oppressed by the devil; for God was with Him.'

There is nothing more important to me, whenever I minister God's Word, than knowing God's anointing. This empowering comes from seeking for the Lord to fill you, being open to the Holy Spirit to do whatever He wants and from recognising your total dependence on Him. Have you ever seen the Holy Spirit as your Senior Partner in ministry? Some Christians are frightened of the Holy Spirit, but, there is nothing to fear. Jesus said that the Holy Spirit will lead you into all truth, He will never lead you into error! Some talk about the Holy Spirit as though He were a doctrine, rather than God, equal with the Father and the Son. The Holy Spirit is not a doctrine to argue about, but God to surrender to. Some ministers have spoken out very unwisely about things that they do not understand concerning the gifts of the Holy Spirit. Ananias and Sapphira were struck down dead for seeking to lie to and disregarding the Holy Spirit (Acts 5:3). When the religious rulers of Jesus' day accused Him of working by the power of Satan, He warned them that blasphemy against the Holy Spirit is the only sin that will not be forgiven. Sin against the Holy Spirit is a very serious thing. It is better to keep quiet rather than to say something against the work of the Spirit. Some people say, 'But what if I surrender to the Holy Spirit and something strange happens? What if I receive some counterfeit gift?' That is a lie propagated by the devil; you cannot receive something bad by surrendering to God. The Holy Spirit will never lead you to do things that are out of line with God's Word. God only gives good gifts to His children (Luke 11:13).

I live in dependence on the Holy Spirit. I want to flow with the Holy Spirit. When I share the gospel before thousands of Muslims and say, 'Don't just take my word for it, God is going to confirm the message that I have shared with signs following', I am dependent on God moving! If God didn't turn up, I would be in serious trouble!

The Holy Spirit is not just some Divine influence or force – He is a Person. He lives within you. The apostle Paul wrote, 'The Grace of our Lord Jesus Christ and the love of God and the fellowship of the Holy Spirit be with you all' (2 Corinthians 13:14). The Holy Spirit wants to fellowship with you. He wants to communicate with you and to show you the Father's will (Acts 10:19,20, Acts 8:29). He wants to lead and to direct you. The apostles wrote to the believers at Antioch, 'It seemed good to the Holy Spirit and to us...' (Acts 15:28). They knew an intimate walk with the Holy Spirit that many today know nothing of.

I believe that there is no greater need for God's servants

today than the anointing of the Holy Spirit. You can have all of the theory, theologically sound doctrines and no power. To go without the power of the Holy Spirit is like trying to drive a car without an engine. Jesus said, 'You shall receive power after the Holy Spirit has come upon you' (Acts 1:8). The Greek word Jesus used for 'power' was *dunamis*, from which we get our English words 'dynamite', 'dynamo' and 'dynamic'. Have you got the 'heavenly dynamite' in your life? We are told to 'walk' in the Spirit, to 'live' in the Spirit and to 'pray' in the Spirit.

If you do not know the power of the Holy Spirit may I encourage you to earnestly seek for the Lord to fill you. The Holy Spirit was freely outpoured at Pentecost and so you can receive right now as you reach out in faith (Luke 11:9–13).

When we truly worship, the presence of God comes down. Then, by faith, people can just reach out and touch the Lord. That is why a lot of people get healed as they worship, for their eyes are off themselves and their needs and onto the Lord.

4. Walk in Obedience to the Lord

We must walk in obedience to the Lord's will, as revealed in His Word. We also need to learn to walk in sensitivity to the Holy Spirit's direction for our lives day by day.

Jesus said, 'I only do the things that My Father shows Me.' We too need that walk of obedience, if we want to be used by Him.

The Bible tells us that the Holy Spirit can be grieved. Paul wrote, 'Do not grieve the Holy Spirit of God, by whom you are sealed for the day of redemption' (Ephesians 4:30). Our total dependence on the Holy Spirit in ministry highlights the importance of maintaining a godly walk with the Lord.

Do not go around laying hands on people if you are not right with God.

5. Take Steps of Faith

A young man came back to the Lord a while ago and after getting right with God, approached one of my colleagues and said, 'How do I start praying for the sick?' He simply replied, 'Find someone who is sick and pray for them!' 'Thanks' said the man and off he went. A few minutes later he returned with his friend, beaming from ear to ear. 'Go on, tell him what happened,' he said excitedly. 'Well' his friend replied, 'I was just standing over there waiting and he said, "Do you need the Lord to heal you of anything?" I told him that I had got a stiff neck. So he laid his hands on me and said "Be healed in Jesus' Name" and I was!"

Don't be afraid to take steps of faith. Early in my ministry, I was fearful of praying for the sick in case nothing happened. This same fear has held many other Christians back too. But, you have got to step out in faith and start somewhere. Early in ministry I felt that the Lord spoke to me and said, 'Healing the sick is not your responsibility. *Ministering to the sick is your response to My ability.*' Ever since then I have just sought to be faithful in ministry. I minister out of God's great ability to heal, not out of who I am.

Just like Peter, we have to get out of the boat and walk on water. That means doing what you have not done before. There is no insurance company that will insure you to walk on water. It is a total risk all the way! You risk sinking, but you also risk walking. So, you have to just get out of the boat! It has often been said that faith is spelt R.I.S.K.

It is no use saying, 'I wish I could minister to people like you do, Peter.' You have got to start where you are right now. This kind of comment reminds me of the story of the person who stopped on their journey to ask for directions. The local person that was asked, looked thoughtful for a moment and then said, 'Go to the end of the road, then turn right down into the village, eh...' Pausing, he continued, 'No, no, turn around and just keep straight on over the hill and eh...' Then, with a puzzled look on his face he added, 'If I were you, I wouldn't start from here.' You **have** to start from here. You have to start from where you are right now.

The German evangelist Reinhard Bonnke's ministry took off, after he had to take a step of faith and believe that God would use him. This was after a visiting evangelist had left the crusade early. With a packed church awaiting, Reinhard had to minister to the sick himself. That night, many were healed and God began a mighty work in the church. Soon afterwards, the Lord called Reinhard to take the message of His saving and healing power across Africa, from Cape Town to Cairo.

Although we must take steps of faith, we must also be realistic about where our own faith level is. I saw the Lord heal my friend's stomach-aches and backpains before I saw blind eyes opened. As I saw God's faithfulness in the small things, so my faith grew to pray for greater needs. Soon, I started praying for some non-Christian friends who were sick. Some of them got healed and as a result were saved. One or two of them did not get instantly healed, but interestingly, they still got saved, because they saw that someone cared.

6. Learn from Others

The Bible mentions several different groups of people who should be involved in ministering healing.

Firstly, Jesus said, 'These signs will follow *them that believe*. In My name they will cast out demons...they will lay hands on the sick and they will recover' (Mark 16:17,18).

Notice that Jesus spoke these words in reference simply to 'them that believe.' The 'signs following' are not limited to apostles, famous preachers or some select group of Christians. If you are a believer, what I am sharing is relevant to you. Believing of course is the key. As you read these words, let your faith rise, that God can use you. Any Christian can be involved in seeing the sick healed.

Secondly, there are some people to whom God has given a special *ministry gift of healing* (1 Corinthians 12:29,30). They are not healers. Jesus is the healer, but they have a high level of faith when it comes to ministering to the sick and an outstanding high number of people are completely healed, often instantly, when they minister.

This gift has often been neglected by the Church. Many in an eagerness to involve the whole Church in ministry to the sick, have failed to learn from those gifted in this area and to first have their own faith built up to see miracles. Thus much 'body ministry' has been done out of 'hope' or 'wishful thinking' rather than faith. This has left many people well prayed for, but disappointed. All the gifts that God has given to the Church are to equip us for ministry. We neglect these gifts to our loss.

As a new Christian I travelled many hundreds of miles to attend conferences and meetings where the sick were being healed. I am so glad that I did. It was there that the scriptures were opened on the subject and my faith grew to expect miracles today. We can learn so much from others that are being effectively used in ministry. Some pastors discourage their members from attending healing services and hide leaflets about such events from them. Often, because of fear, they disapprove of their members going to meetings outside their own church events. But if these ministers do not open their pulpits to such ministries that God has given to the Church they cannot blame their people for going elsewhere. Such gifts are obviously very necessary, or God would have not given them to the Church. To reject these gifts can be to reject Christ's healing.

It is vital that we attend churches and events where our faith will be uplifted. It is also good to read books that will build our confidence in God's Word.

Thirdly, *the elders of the church.* James wrote, 'Is any among you sick? Let him call for the elders of the church and let them pray over him and anoint him with oil in the Name of the Lord and the prayer of faith will save the sick and the Lord will raise him up and if he has committed any sin he will be forgiven' (James 5:14,15). God's intention is that all church leaders should be men of faith, who are actively involved in ministry to the sick. He desires that such faith-filled ministry be readily available to every believer.

Fourthly, *pioneer ministries,* such as evangelists and apostles. In the Book of Acts, wherever the early Church leaders went advancing the gospel, the sick were healed. The Lord confirmed His Word with signs following. It was His 'Amen' to the message that they shared. In pioneer evangelism, I firmly believe that miracles in Jesus' Name are the key to a breakthrough among the unreached.

7. Realise that God Wants the Person to be Well

In heaven there is no sickness, no lack, no disease, no poverty and no hurt relationships; this is God's perfect will for His people.

It is vital, if we hope to be used in ministry, that we realise Satan is the author of sickness and that God wants people well, otherwise our prayers will be full of doubt and consequently ineffective. You will not be healed while you believe that it is God's will that you are sick. As we have seen, it is 'the prayer of faith that saves the sick' and not just prayer.

We have seen in earlier chapters that God is on the side of health. He tells us, 'Beloved I wish above all things that thou mayest be in health and prosper even as thy soul prospers' (3 John 2). He wants us to be as physically well as we are spiritually well. Although we realise that there are possible blockages to healing and that not everyone is healed instantly, this should not shake our faith that God wants people well.

I used to have warts all over my right wrist. I had tried getting rid of them with various liquids and had even been to the doctor to have them burnt off. Yet they returned. After I became a Christian I heard that God healed, but I had no faith that He would heal me. I could not even imagine God doing it. It was as if the enemy kept saying, 'It's only your vanity that wants to get rid of them and there are a lot of people worse off than you'. It is amazing how this attitude, 'There are a lot of people worse off than me,' stops people coming for ministry. Actually, it is an insult to God, for it is implying that if He uses His power meeting your little needs, He might not have enough left for people's bigger needs!

One day I was in a meeting where a little girl came forward to testify. 'I had a wart on my knee,' she said, 'and Jesus has healed me'. As she said that, my faith took off. I thought, 'If Jesus could heal her, he could heal me'. I already knew from God's Word that He wanted me healed, but this was the boost that my faith needed. I got out of my seat and went for ministry. The next morning when I woke up I did not have a single wart on my arm, they had all gone. To this day, the only mark I have on my arm is a burn mark from where the doctor had failed to burn them off. I am sure that God always wanted to heal me, but it was not until my faith was released that I received my healing.

8. Build Faith in Those to Whom You are Ministering

Ministers who do not preach Christ the healer do their people a great injustice. They leave them wide open to all the attacks of the enemy. When we preach the Word, faith replaces unbelief and people come for prayer expectantly (Romans 10:17).

A lot of Christians pray for what they would 'like' to see God do, rather than what they really believe God is going to do. They pray out of exuberance, enthusiasm or wishful thinking, rather than out of a faith that is grounded on the Word of God.

Building faith in those you are ministering to is so important. We have already seen how faith was evident when Jesus healed people. He said such things as: 'Your faith has made you whole' (Matthew 9:22); 'According to your faith be it done unto you' (Matthew 9:27) and 'As you have believed, so it shall be done to you' (Matthew 9:13).

If faith were not necessary we could walk in and empty hospital wards, but faith is essential.

During a crusade in Oxford, I agreed to visit a woman who had been bedridden for three weeks and was in great pain. She was hardly able to move due to a back problem. I asked this lady, 'Do you believe that God wants you healed and that He is going to heal you?' She replied, 'The vicar has already prayed for me and so has...' and with that she listed the names of many others. 'Well' I said, 'I don't just want to add my name to the list, so I will pray a general prayer and leave.' This made her think and begin to reach out to the Lord to do something. I shared some faith-building truths from God's Word, until she said, 'Now, I believe that God wants to heal me.' I spoke the words, 'In Jesus' Name I rebuke these back problems and I tell them to go. Be healed in the Name of Jesus!' I then said to her, 'I will now leave the room so that you can move around. Then if you give me a call I will come back.' In a matter of seconds, instead of calling, the door opened and there the woman stood in her dressing gown, with a big smile on her face. She bent over and touched her toes, saying, 'I am healed.'

When her husband returned home that evening, to his suprise, she was up, dressed and cooking a meal for him. Her friend later sent me a copy of the church magazine with her testimony in it. The important thing to notice is that the breakthrough occurred when she went from wishful thinking ('it would be nice to be healed') to expectant faith.

When there are a line of people in a meeting coming for prayer, I will often look to see who seems to have faith for healing and pray for them first. Their healing will encourage others. It often shows on people's faces whether or not they are expecting God to do anything. We read in the Book of Acts, that after the lame man had heard Paul speak, 'Paul, observing him intently and *seeing that he had faith to be healed,* said with a loud voice, "stand up straight on your feet!" and he leapt and walked' (Acts 14:9,10).

Build faith in those you are ministering to. Share faith-building truths from God's Word to dispel their doubts and to lift their expectancy. Share testimonies of what God has done in your own life. That is why the final section of this book contains photographic reports from some of our crusades around the world. We trust that they will encourage you to see that Jesus is the same today and to step out in faith in a greater way. That is why we take a video camera to our crusades, so that we can bring back records of the miracles as they happen, for many in our land have not seen mighty miracles before.

I think it is important to add here, that there is a big difference between using these truths to build people's faith and using them to condemn others. A lot of precious people, for example, who are crippled or seriously ill, have been hurt by insensitive Christians who have said such things as, 'the reason you are not healed is because you have not got enough faith.' This saddens me so much. When it comes to lack of faith, it is not just the faith of certain individuals, it is all of our faith in general that needs to be lifted.

There are some Christians who are always pressurising

others to go forward for prayer at every opportunity. If they see someone in a wheelchair, they always say, 'You should go up for prayer.' However, I believe that it is best to leave people to respond when they want to and when they have faith rising in their hearts to be healed. Otherwise they will only get disappointed. It is better that they can just peacefully hear the Word over and over until they themselves believe that they are ready to go for ministry.

I usually ask people when they come for prayer, 'What are you believing for God to do?' There is a big difference between 'What are you believing for God to do?' and 'What do you want God to do?' This helps me find out where people's faith is. 'Well, I would love to be healed, but I am not sure,' some answer. I will then often encourage them to listen to a tape or read a book that will point them towards the promises in God's Word and then to return for prayer afterwards. It was when Paul 'perceived that he had faith to be healed' that he commanded the man crippled from birth to 'stand upright on your feet' and the man leaped and walked (Acts 14:8–10). Sometimes it is better to agree in prayer for something that they can believe for, than to pray in doubt and unbelief.

As a pastor I always preferred to minister to people straight after preaching the Word, for it is the preaching of the Word that releases people's faith to receive from God. So now I give those present an opportunity to receive prayer and ministry each time I preach. I have found that people receive far more when I minister this way. When a pastor arranges to meet someone later on during the week, he will often find that by the time he gets there, the urgency of the situation has worn off. The cares of the world have often robbed people of the Word and of their expectation. Praying straight after you have ministered the Word seals something in people's hearts. When you minister after having lifted up Jesus, you will find that people are looking to the Lord to meet their needs. I have often found in long mid-week counselling sessions that people come looking to the pastor to meet their needs. This is, of course, not to say that there is no place for on-going ministry, however, I have found that a hundred times more happens when you minister straight after lifting people's faith. One characteristic I have noticed of the rapidly-growing Churches in the world, is that each week the people know that they can bring the unsaved to the services and that they will hear the gospel and have an opportunity to receive ministry.

9. Help People to Release their Faith

Our goal is to see God's power released to meet the needs of those to whom we are ministering. In the account of the crippled lady who touched the hem of Jesus' garment, we read that as she did, 'power went out from Him and healed her.' Her touch of faith released the flow of God's power.

There are a number of means recorded in the scriptures whereby God's power was released. For example, Jesus touched people, He put His fingers in a man's ears, He put some moist clay on a blind man's eyes and He spoke to them. These were each specific things. They were very real and practical actions. They were 'points of contact' between Jesus and the person who needed healing.

In the Book of Acts, we read that even after the shadow of Peter's body fell upon the sick, they were healed and delivered (Acts 5:15).

In Acts 19:11,12, handkerchiefs were taken from Paul and laid upon the sick and they were healed. There was no healing power in Paul's handkerchiefs, but they became a means to help the sick release their faith.

The laying-on of hands, prayer and anointing with oil, do not bring the healing. They are simply the means to release our faith.

If I suggested that we went out for a meal, it would remain just a good idea unless we set a time and a place to meet up. If we just said, 'We could meet together anytime and any place'; the chances of us meeting would be very small. The same is true of much praying, it is very vague. The laying-on of hands, for example, sets the time to release our faith where we say, 'Lord, we are believing for healing right now.'

As we lay hands on a person at that moment we agree together for their healing. 'Be healed now, in Jesus' Name.'

Jesus said, 'If two of you shall *agree* on earth as touching anything that they ask, it shall be done for them by my Father in heaven' (Matthew 18:19). We need to find a point at which we can agree and for which we both have faith. I often encourage people by saying, 'When I lay hands on you, at that moment let us release our faith together to receive your healing'.

There are other ways of helping people to release their faith. The spoken word is another way. The centurion said to Jesus, 'Only speak the word and my servant will be healed' (Matthew 8:8). There is power in the word spoken in faith. It is significant that there are no biblical accounts of Christ praying for the sick. He usually just spoke healing to the person; 'Be made whole,' or, 'Rise, take up your bed and walk.' He commanded the condition to be well (Luke 4:39; 5:13; 7:6–10) or the spirit to leave (Luke 4:35) or the person being healed to do something as a step of faith (Luke 5:24; 6:10; 7:14).

There are a few cases where the scriptures do not tell us specifically that faith was present. However, to suggest that faith was not present simply because the word is omitted is unwise. This is shown particularly where different gospel writers carry the same account of a healing and where faith is mentioned by some of the authors and not by others. For example, Matthew does not mention the faith that was present at the healing of Jairus' daughter, only Mark mentions the faith present at the healing of the epileptic demoniac and only Matthew accounts for the faith present at the healing of the Canaanite woman's daughter although the other writers carry the accounts.

The main way that faith is released to receive healing is by hearing the Word of God preached. 'Faith comes by hearing and hearing by the Word of God' (Romans 10:17).

I do not preach on Christ's healing power because people get healed, I preach it out of obedience to God's Word. If no-one was saved in my meetings I would still preach forgiveness, because it is so clear in the Bible. Yet, it seems sad to me that those who claim to believe that the Bible is 'authoritative in all matters of faith and conduct', ignore the wealth of scriptural teaching on healing, the laying on of hands and anointing.

Ministering healing is not having an experience and then going to the Bible to find support. It is standing on the promises of God's Word until our experience catches up. Most pastors have had to preach on Christ's healing power and to deal with the doubts and unbelief in their congregation for sometime before they have seen a breakthrough. At a recent conference where I was one of the speakers, a well-known preacher shared that for the first ten months after he saw the place of healing and miracles in the Word of God and began to preach on them, no one was healed. Then, one by one, people began to be healed. After about three years his church began to see the sick healed on a regular basis and, as a result, several thousand came to Christ.

> Jesus went about all the cities and villages, *teaching* in their synagogues and *preaching* the gospel of the Kingdom and *healing* every sickness and every disease among the people. Matthew 9:35

> His fame travelled and a great multitude came together to *hear* and to be *healed* of their infirmities. Luke 5:15

> A great multitude of people out of all Judea and Jerusalem and from the sea coast of Tyre and Sidon, which came to *hear* Him and to be *healed* of their diseases. Luke 6:17

Notice that teaching and preaching came before healing. Many people today just want to arrive at the meeting and dash forward for prayer. A lot of people want to be healed, but they don't want to hear God's Word first. Such people seldom receive anything from God. It is by hearing the Word that we receive the faith to be healed.

Some people say to a friend, 'Get them to pray for me, I do not have time to go to the meeting.' Yet they will spend hours in hospital or waiting in the doctor's surgery. As one preacher put it, 'They have got time to die, but they have not got time to receive ministry.' I do believe in praying for those who are too sick to attend the service and have seen many healed this way. However, I will usually encourage those who come on behalf of others to take some faith-building material or a tape of the service back to their friend. It is always best to bring people to the meeting where they can hear God's Word and where people are expecting miracles. In the gospels and the Book of Acts, it is interesting to note how often people brought their friends on their beds.

As I have already said, there is a place for coming for prayer on behalf of others; many have been healed this way, especially children, whose parents have come on their behalf. In Part Three I will share the lovely story of the Tanzanian Government official's son who was at the point of death and was healed when the man came seeking help. In the scriptures we have such examples as Jairus who came on behalf of his daughter and the Centurion who came on behalf of his servant. However, I have found that those who are healed this way are themselves usually believing for a healing, rather than being too lazy or too unbelieving to attend. It is rare that adults are healed this way who will not make some step towards God. People often seek prayer for their unsaved relatives. The first question I usually ask is, 'Do they know that you are requesting prayer for them?' If the unsaved person requested prayer, we have a point at which to release our faith. If not, my main prayer will be that they will come to know the Lord and to see their need for Jesus. Most people that receive healing have taken a first step towards God.

One of the funniest times of praying on behalf of others was at a meeting in England where the Lord gave me some Words of Knowledge, and on each occasion someone said, 'That's my wife' or 'That's my husband. He is counselling in the counselling room.' I wondered what the Lord was doing, but, when all the people returned from the counselling room we called forward the various ones who the words of knowledge had been for and each one testified how as they were praying with others, they had been healed! It was as if the

Lord was saying, 'Because they are serving Me, they are not going to miss out.'

10. Be Open to the Lord for Further Information

Ask the Lord to show you if there are any blockages to the person being healed and be open to the Lord to highlight any resentment, fear, unbelief, inner hurts, past occult involvement, unconfessed sin or anxiety, that might hinder the flow of God's power. Often, until people are willing to let go of such things, they cannot be healed. Divine healing is more than just getting physically well. It includes a total healing of our relationships with God, ourselves and with others. It is healing for our emotions as well as for our ailments.

During one crusade a woman was brought to the front bent and crippled with arthritis. As she came forward, I felt the Lord say to me, 'Ask her who she resents.' 'Who is it that you resent?', I asked. Her friend said, 'Go on, tell him.' She mentioned a man's name. I said, 'Will you forgive him, because your resentment is completely destroying your health.' 'I could never forgive him,' she replied. I explained how Jesus had said that in order to be forgiven, we must forgive and how her sin had hurt Jesus far more than she had been hurt, yet Jesus wanted to forgive her. I asked her again if she would forgive the man. 'I forgive you,' she said, naming the person. As she said that the power of God hit her and she stood up straight, completely healed by the Lord. I didn't have to even pray for healing: when the blockage was out of the way, she was healed.

So, be sensitive to the Lord's voice, that He might give you further information to help you minister effectively and to highlight any possible blockages in those receiving their healing.

So, let me summarise these points:

1. Recognise and emphasise that Jesus is the healer
2. Check your motives
3. See your need of the Lord's anointing
4. Walk in obedience to the Lord
5. Take steps of faith
6. Learn from others

7. Realise that God wants the person well
8. Build faith in those to whom you are ministering
9. Help people to release their faith
10. Be open to the Lord for further information

16 TO BOLDLY GO WHERE NO MAN'S GONE BEFORE

'This gospel of the Kingdom must be preached in all the world as a witness to all the nations and then the end will come.'
Matthew 24:14

Some say that the Bible is outdated.

I believe that God's Word is more up-to-date than the daily papers. Our God is the Alpha and Omega. In fact, when you read Matthew chapter twenty-four, you could be reading the daily paper!

Jesus' disciples had asked Him, 'What will be the sign of your coming and of the end of the age?' Jesus, in response, listed false christs, wars, rumours of wars, famines, earthquakes, persecution, false prophets and lawlessness as the signs to watch out for. All of these are on the increase and are happening simultaneously in our day.

However, the key to the passage is verse fourteen, for it includes the words 'and then the end will come'.

And then

> 'And this gospel of the Kingdom must be preached in all the world as a witness to all the nations *and then* the end will come.' Matthew 24:14

When I first became a Christian I heard sermons on the Second Coming. We were told that Jesus was coming soon and so we sat waiting. We longed for Christ's return but we never once, as a church, went out to share the gospel with those who had never heard. We never prayed fervently together or gave sacrificially to send missionaries to the unreached nations. We had missed the challenge of this verse; it should never cause us just to sit waiting; it should stir us to rise up and take the gospel to our world.

Maybe we thought that the job had been done. But it has not.

Maybe, because we had heard the gospel, we assumed that everyone else had heard the message of Christ too. But they have not.

There are over five billion people alive on planet earth at this time, yet over 2.2 billion of them have never heard the message of God's love.

We talk about the Second Coming, when nearly half our world has not heard about His First Coming. In 110 cities of the world, one missionary works among one million people or more!

In Britain there is an average of one full-time Christian worker to every 500 people. That is excluding deacons, elders, home group leaders and the numerous lay ministries in our churches!

How selfish we can be with the ministries, finance and resources that God has given us. Isn't it unbelievable that around 95% of church finances from tithes and offerings are spent internally, on those who already know the Lord, while nearly half the world has still not heard the gospel?

Amazingly some Christians dismiss the challenge of mission by saying, 'Why go to the ends of the earth with the gospel when there are still unreached people in our own towns?'

Most people in Britain could get up and walk a few hundred yards to a church, if they wished. Almost half the world has no such opportunity. Does God love British people more than the millions of Asians who have never had an opportunity to hear of His love? As Dr Oswald Smith put it, 'Why should anyone hear the gospel twice before others have heard it once?'

Are you not glad that the early Church did not have this attitude, of keeping the message to itself? If it had we would still be lost!

I speak at Asian gospel outreach events where up to 60,000 Muslims gather to hear the message of Christ. Several thousand often respond to give their lives to Him. Our world has never been so reachable. Those who have never heard the message of Jesus before are eagerly turning to Him.

> How shall they believe in Him of whom they have not heard? And how shall they hear without a preacher? And how shall they preach except they be sent? Romans 10:14,15

At Reach Out Ministries we are primarily seeking to target the unreached people of our world. They need to hear the message of Christ. Should we not do all that we can to send the gospel to them? I go to some tribes, where they drink Coca-Cola, but they've never heard about Jesus! In one sense it is amusing to see tribal people with a stick or spear in one hand and a bottle of Coke in the other. Yet it is also very tragic. Do Coca-Cola believe in their product more than the Church in its commission from Jesus? Isn't it unbelievable that in one hundred years Coke is available all over the world? Yet it is two thousand years since Christ told us to take the gospel to the whole world and we still haven't obeyed Him!

In the 1940s the owners of Coca-Cola made a strategic decision to re-invest a very large percentage of their profits in opening up new plants all over the world. The goal was that wherever American troops were in the world, they should be able to buy a bottle of Coke. Consequently, now one in every three soft drinks purchased in the world bears the name 'Coca Cola.' Where is such strategic planning in the Church? Where is that commitment to 'boldly go where no man's gone before'?

Jesus said, 'This gospel of the Kingdom must be preached in all the world as a witness to all the nations and then shall the end come.'

Do you long to see Jesus' return? Do you long to see Him reigning? Then do all you can to reach this world for Christ!

This verse will have us going!
This verse will have us sending others!
This verse will have us giving!
This verse will have us praying!

I believe that the lack of strategy, sacrificial giving and putting of mission first, are the main reason why Jesus' Great Commission remains uncompleted.

I believe that reaching the unreached **must become** the Church's priority.

Must be

> 'And this gospel of the Kingdom *must be* preached in all the world as a witness to all the nations and then the end will come.' Matthew 24:14

Jesus said this gospel of the Kingdom **must** be preached in all the world.

Why 'must' it be?

1) Because God loves the world
2) Because hell is a reality
3) Because God desires not the death of a sinner
4) Because He does not want any to perish, but all to have the opportunity to accept the Saviour
5) Because it is appointed unto man once to die and after that face the judgement.

Is this not enough reason why this gospel of the Kingdom **must** be preached in all the world?

Are these not reason enough why we **must** do all that we can to send the gospel to the ends of the earth?

This gospel

> 'And *this gospel* of the Kingdom must be preached in all the world as a witness to all nations and then the end will come.' Matthew 24:14

Finally, Jesus said, 'This gospel'.

It is 'this gospel' that must be preached, 'this gospel of the Kingdom'. Not just any gospel.

When Jesus said, 'This gospel', His disciples would have known of no other gospel than the one which they had seen and heard and witnessed.

> Jesus went around all Galilee teaching in their synagogues, preaching the gospel of the Kingdom and healing every sickness and every disease among the people.
> Matthew 9:35

The gospel of the Kingdom includes healing and miracles. Jesus is King over disease and sickness and the power of sin.

Jesus said 'This gospel of the Kingdom must be preached *as a witness*' – literally, with evidence – with signs following. We have seen the unsaved turn to Christ in their thousands when they see the miracles in Jesus Name.

Our God has not changed.

Still today God confirms His Word with signs following (Mark 16:15–20).

It is this gospel of the Kingdom which 'must be preached in all the nations as a witness, and then shall the end come.'

SOME ALARMING FIGURES

* Of the 5 billion people in our world 2.2 billion have never heard the message of Christ
* Most of the unreached live in one of five main people groups – the Muslims, the Buddhists, the Hindus, tribal people and the Chinese
* There are only 5,000 missionaries working among the three main people groups (Muslims, Hindus, Buddhists)
* There are 110 cities in our world where there is just one missionary to one million people
* Each day 80,000 people enter a Christless eternity

Jesus said 'Go into all the world and preach the gospel to *every* creature' (Mark 16:15).

PART THREE
CRUSADE REPORTS

These reports from some of Reach Out Ministries' crusades are a living testimony to the fact that Jesus Christ is the same yesterday, today and forever. (Hebrews 13:8)

HEAD HUNTERS TURN TO CHRIST

As the battered bus spluttered around the dirt roads and steep mountain ridges, on our eight hour journey to Bontoc, I began to ask, 'What have I let myself in for?'

I thought back to earlier in the year when a minister from Bontoc had attended one of our Crusades and asked me to visit the tribe. He explained that they were ancestral spirit worshippers and a head-hunting tribe. They were at war with two other tribes and when one murder took place, nineteen lives were expected to be taken in exchange. He was one of the few converts to Christianity there and had started a small church. He explained that because of the location, no evangelists ever visited and that they had never had a crusade there in the history of the town. Yet, he believed that at least a quarter of the tribe would attend if I would come.

The bus continued its journey around the narrow track, just wide enough for one vehicle, revealing the sheer 2,000 foot drop. For the thirteen hour journey there were no barriers at the side of the road and many times the wheels got agonisingly close to the edge. A magazine article about the journey had referred to it as, 'One of the most uncomfortable and terrifying bus journeys in the world' and warned that buses and vehicles regularly went over the edge.

We continued the climb, reaching the highest point in the Philippines, over 7,000 feet above sea level, overlooking a breathtaking twenty-mile wide valley of rice terraces, hewn out of the mountainside some two thousand years ago. If all of these terraces were put together, they would stretch a quarter of the way around the world!

In a predominantly Roman Catholic country, even the Spanish had failed to reach these ancestral-worshipping

tribes. Only this century a few American Anglican (Episcopal) missionaries had managed to penetrate the mountainous terrain. Nevertheless the people continued to be active head-hunters until very recently, with tribal killings still regularly taking place.

On the first evening as I looked out on the vast crowds that had gathered, I began to wonder what God had in store. As you will see from the reports of others, we were in for a mighty move of God.

The first night the people held back and very few came for salvation.

So, the next day we entered into spiritual warfare, binding the powers of darkness that had ruled here for so long and loosing the people to respond to God and to be saved. I felt the Lord say that there would be a breakthrough and He reminded me of places in the scriptures where whole towns, cities and communities turned to Christ. 'Why not today?' I thought.

That night the power of God came down!

The Anglican Bishop for the mountain regions, Bishop Longrid, attended the crusade. He was a godly man who had

faithfully prayed for a breakthrough here for many years. After the second night's meeting he told us that over three-quarters of the town had attended the meeting and over half of the tribe had came forward to give their lives to Christ! He fell on his knees and joined these people for whom he had faithfully prayed for a breakthrough, as they gave their lives to Christ.

The counsellors and ministers that we had brought with us were vastly outnumbered as hundreds came for salvation.

Over three-quarters of the town had attended the meeting and over half of the tribe had come forward to give their lives to Christ!

A woman walked three hours through the mountains to bring her blind husband to the meeting.

Bishop Longrid joined the hundreds of tribal people as they knelt to give their lives to Christ.

He received his sight and both were saved. The man testified publicly, 'I was blind, but as Peter took his hands away from my eyes I began to see. Now I can see everything clearly.'

One crippled old lady who had walked to the meeting bent over; stood up straight and handed her walking stick to Peter saying, 'I don't need this anymore, you can keep it!'

A year later, up to 1,000 people a night were still attending the follow-up meetings!

The video *A Year of Great Blessing* features some of the miracles and blessings at Bontoc and at other crusades and is available from Reach Out Ministries.

A REPORT FROM THE REV WILLIAM TODCOR

Crusade co-ordinator and local Pastor

The crusade was marvellous!

It was the first such event here. Everyone was saying 'No one will come,' including many of the Christians. But as you'll see on the video 'A Year of Great Blessing', the plaza was packed. Despite opposition from one of the local officials and a constant tearing down of the posters by some people, God moved in power and filled the plaza.

Over three quarters of the town's people came and over half of the town received Jesus. We are so thrilled that God is moving today. We know that the people will go on with the Lord, for this was a real move of the Holy Spirit.

We are so glad that our brother Peter came to this remote place to bring the love of Christ.

Rev William L. Todcor

A REPORT FROM THE REV ANDREW KETTLE

Local Missionary

I have accompanied Peter since his arrival in the Philippines with crusades in Baguio and La Trinidad. I have witnessed amazing signs and wonders, the blind receiving their sight, limbs being restored, deaf ears opened and many people giving their lives to Jesus.

The most amazing miracles took place among the pagan mountain people of Bontoc. Over half of the population of Bontoc gave their lives to Jesus and on the last night we lost count of how many blind received their sight (I know of at least four). Many deaf were healed. Again I lost count of how many cripples discarded their sticks and canes. I have never seen anything like this before!

There has been a change in the town. Beforehand the Bontoc people were known to be reserved and never smiled. Now everyone here smiles, waves and is happy.

As the crusade service started the skies lit up. At first I wondered if we were going to have thunder, but no, it was as if it was a sign from the Lord, as if a break-through had happened in the heavenlies, as the principalities and powers that have ruled here were defeated.

The Anglican Bishop came to see me after the crusade absolutely amazed at what had happened. He had never seen anything like it in his life and he is an elderly man. He kept thanking Peter for coming.

Rev Andrew Kettle

Many Christians in the West find it hard to believe in miracles, but we saw these things with our own eyes. Bontoc will never be the same again.

40,000 MUSLIMS HEAR GOOD NEWS!

40,000 people gathered to hear the Good News of Jesus Christ in the Islamic Republic of Pakistan.

This was a truly unique event in this Islamic State where turning to Christ can lead to great persecution, rejection from one's family and even imprisonment.

Yet, despite the government spies present each night, taking back reports, over 10,000 people made a public stand to give their lives to Christ and hundreds of Bibles were distributed in Urdu, the national language.

So why did Peter and the team receive such an amazing opportunity to share the message of Christ?

One of the keys was the amazing miracles that took place in answer to prayer.

Peter preaching in Pakistani clothes

The Islamic papers carried the front page headline 'MIRACLES' with photographs and a report of the eyewitness accounts made by the Muslim reporter. He wrote, 'I have seen it with my own eyes, the blind are seeing, the deaf are hearing and the crippled are walking.' The papers also told the story of a woman who had been insane for fourteen years and had been brought forty miles to the meetings by her family. After prayer she was set free and testified in her right mind.

As the word travelled, night by night the crowds grew.

Many came to encounter Jesus as healer and left having met with Him as Saviour!

The photo above is not of the crowd (the camera flash was not powerful enough to record the vast crowd). These in the photograph are just the ones that sat in front of the seating barriers in the 'no sitting' area!

A Senior Muslim Government official came secretly to the hotel to receive prayer. Afterwards Peter told him that he needed to read the Bible to discover who Jesus really is. The man said, 'Secretly I already do'.

After praying from the platform for the sick, people who had been healed were invited to come and to testify to what God had done.

In seconds a massive crowd gathered.

Dr Naeem, a qualified medical doctor, was on hand each night to check people's healings before they spoke.

In one meeting alone, four blind people testified that they had received their sight.

Only eternity will reveal all that God did, but what a wonderful opportunity to share the gospel with 40,000 Muslims in an Islamic State!

A Muslim Police Inspector testifies 'My Mother has been healed.'

A man testified that he has been completely healed of arthritis.

A cross-eyed girl is healed.

A blind girl told how she has received her sight.

IN TANZANIA...

THE BLIND SEE, THE DEAF HEAR, THE LAME WALK AND THE POOR HAVE THE GOOD NEWS PREACHED TO THEM

The words spoken by Jesus in Luke 7:19–22, sum up Peter's visit to Tanzania in East Africa. Night by night the Central Hall was packed, with most of the seats being taken two hours before the meetings began. Others flowed out into the foyer and onto the streets.

During the crusade 3,507 people responded publicly, the majority making commitments to Christ. The President of Tanzania even requested tapes of Peter's messages every night and his personal assistant, who travels the world with him, was in each meeting.

The team met many people who had received Christ during Peter's previous crusades in Tanzania. One young man, who had been saved during the 1983 Dar-Es-Salaam crusade, had gone back to his tribe and immediately led others to the Lord. He had started a church in his village where there had been no prior Christian witness.

A Mighty Outpouring

The final night of the crusade was a real highlight, with the believers from many different churches linking up across the hall and praying for unity. As the team walked home that night through the streets, they witnessed conversations taking place about the Lord everywhere as the whole city seemed alive with excited Christians. Large crowds at the bus stops were singing and praising as they waited for the buses.

Many attended from the various colleges and universities. It was an amazing opportunity for Peter to share the gospel with the future leaders, politicians and teachers in the land, many of whom surrendered their lives to the Lord. For example, over a quarter of one teacher training college were converted during the crusade. Imagine the excitement of the believers there! Beforehand, there had only been six Christians. At the next college Christian Union meeting over a quarter of the students attended!

One man, Peter Miranda, shared how he had been saved during Peter's previous Dar-Es-Salaam crusade. At the time he was an alcoholic sailor, but the Lord completely set him free. He shared his exciting testimony of how the Lord had since called him into full-time Christian work.

Peter Miranda is just one of the many lives transformed there.

Some of the Testimonies Given at the Dar-Es-Salaam Crusade

'I received Christ at home after the meeting and slept peacefully for the first time'...'My brother-in-law was saved and my neighbour received Christ during the crusade'... 'All of my children got saved!'...'My brother met with the Lord. I had been praying for him for years'...'My two children, who were sick at home, were healed as Peter prayed for them in the meeting.'

Miracles

As well as the great numbers who responded to receive Christ, hundreds of other sick folk were healed. One night seven blind people said that they had received their sight, six of whom came back the next night and testified publicly. Many deaf people also shared that they had been healed in Jesus' Name.

A little boy who had been dumb from birth spoke for the first time in his life and was also healed of a paralysed arm and hand. As a result of this miracle his Muslim grandmother was converted to Christ and threw away the potions given her by the witch doctor. She also discarded her black Muslim robe and returned to the Crusade looking radiant in a beautiful white gown with flowers all over it.

Another man was healed of a terrible stutter and spoke perfectly. Others, who publicly testified to receiving healing, included a professor from the local University, the Army Colonel in charge of the Tanzanian Tank Division and the Assistant Chief Commissioner of Police (number three in the nation). He was healed of a 20-year back condition caused by a car accident and shared publicly that after being healed, he had slept perfectly and without pain.

Government Official's Son Healed

After the close of one meeting, a very troubled senior Government official came and asked Peter to pray for his young son, who was at the point of death in hospital. It is very rare for a small child who gets malaria to live. Straight after Peter had prayed with him, the man returned to the hospital, to be met by some very shocked hospital staff. His son was sitting up in bed, playing with his toys, having already eaten a meal. The child was dismissed and the grateful father returned to the rally the next night to describe the miracle that had taken place.

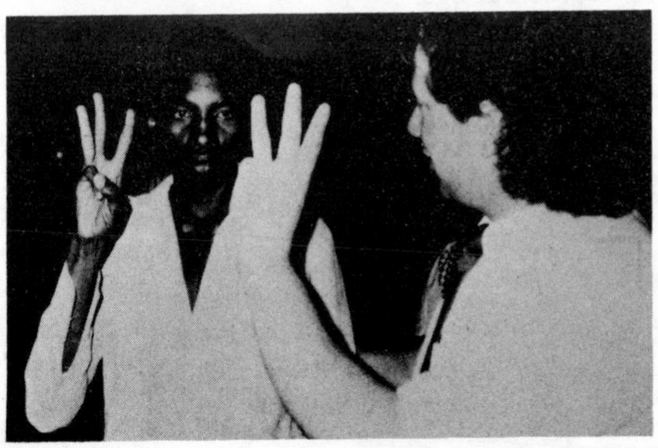

Siriri Echeni – one of several blind men healed during the Dar-Es-Saalam Crusade

A LETTER FROM JOHN NKANDA

The Tanzanian Crusade Co-ordinator

Dear Peter,

Our follow-up committee has been giving good reports of people who were saved coming to church and going on well.

A person who had heard of the crusade on the radio got saved one night and when we sent a letter to him, as one of our follow-up methods, he came to church at my Kimara fellowship and gave a very exciting testimony of how God had changed his life. This person said that he had started to witness about Christ to the people in the area where he lives. The result is that many have been saved through his testimony. We went there and have now planted a church there also. This is one of several new churches that have resulted from the witnessing of the converts from the crusade.

Churches also report of receiving hundreds of new members from the crusade.

I am excited by the fact that God is using you to bring a great revival to our age.

Rev John Nkanda

A REPORT FROM THE REV DEREK BOND

Muslims Turn to Christ

After the Dar-Es-Salaam crusade we visited a densely populated Muslim area nearby. On the way to the crusade, the organisers told us that the last group of Christians to have gone there were stoned!

After Peter had preached, he gave an appeal for people to receive Christ and only three Muslim women came forward.

It is a big thing in a Muslim community for people to give their lives to Christ and often marks them out for persecution. Instantly, on seeing her come forward, the husband of one of the women grabbed her and dragged her back into the crowd.

The second night there was a real break-through. Not only did the Muslim woman come forward again, but her husband came too!

After that, Muslim men, in their distinctive gowns and hats, responded to receive Christ every night and many hundreds were counselled during the mission there.

I will never forget how after Peter had preached, one of the Elders of the town took off his Muslim hat and threw it to the ground. Then, after giving his heart to Jesus, he began to jump up and down on it! I had tears in my eyes and still do when I think of it.

Several thousand people gathered each night to hear the message of Christ. They were everywhere, like ants. They were up the trees, hanging from them, on the roofs of the mud huts, all listening intently to the message of the gospel. It was exciting to see these Muslim people who had come from miles around to hear about Jesus!

A church was started in the area at the end of the crusade, with a pastor who had successfully planted new churches in other Muslim areas being brought in to lead the work.

I have travelled with Peter for over fifteen years now and so appreciate him, as do Christians all around the world, for his heart of love for people.

Rev Derek Bond

A WELCOME TO UGANDA

A welcome to Uganda from Dr Samson Kisseka, the Prime Minister (left) and Hon. Balaki Kirya, the Minister of State (right). Praying with Mayanja Nkangi, the ex-Prime Minister who is largely responsible for the economic rebuilding of the country (below).

MIRACLES IN THE PUNJAB

Some of those saved in Peter's last crusade in the country travelled to the meetings to report of new churches started where there had been no previous Christian witness and of many baptisms taking place.

It is good to know that those saved in Peter's past crusades are going on with God.

People arriving at the meetings in and on the buses!

A REPORT FROM

Dr Israel C. Naeem:

What an amazing event!

There was no place to move as thousands crammed into the meetings.

Over 14,500 came to hear the Word of God and around 10,000 responded to know Jesus as their Saviour.

We were so thrilled – and this is a Muslim area and not a Christian one!

I am a medical doctor and I witnessed some amazing miracles of healing in Jesus' Name.

Also, when the people turned to Christ, they discarded their charms given to them by the witchcraft 'pirs'. After the meeting the team burned these charms (Acts 19:18–20).

The final night was wonderful, as many were filled with the Holy Spirit. This has never happened here before.

How we thank God for moving in such a mighty way.

Dr Israel C. Naeem

A REPORT FROM VAUGHAN ALLEN

Reach Out Ministries

As we walked into the meeting I couldn't believe my eyes. There were thousands of people. The whole building was packed!

We slowly picked our way through the crowd to the platform. The atmosphere was electric – people had come expecting miracles.

At the start of the crusade we had experienced some real opposition. The Muslim priests had torn down most of the posters and banners and bodyguards had been assigned to us due to the threat of attack.

But, 'He who is in us is greater than he who is in the world!' Our meeting place was packed to overflowing.

I was standing taking photographs at the back and after taking four or five, I looked around. I was stuck in the crowd because so many new people had arrived. All the people sitting around me laughed because they knew that I could not move.

The Kingdom of God was advanced as many sicknesses were healed. The blind saw, the deaf heard and the large majority of the crowd responded to give their lives to Christ.

There was great excitement at the front of the stage as people pushed and shoved to testify of what God had done. I saw one father smiling with joy as he held up his child who had been deaf and dumb from birth. The little boy had heard and spoken after Jesus had touched him.

A previously blind woman not used to seeing bright lights with her new eyesight, asked for the video camera light to be turned away as she counted the fingers on Peter's hand.

Someone had said to me, 'When you go to the crusade can you confirm to us that the testimonies of amazing miracles are true?' I can say, YES. Amazing, but true!

To tell others that there is a God who cares and to see

hope in people's faces in a hopeless world is an experience I shall never forget. It is good news!

Vaughan Allen

A REPORT FROM PASTOR NAZIR MASIH

Crusade Organiser

Due to the massive crowds, the buses arrived packed to capacity. Even the roofs were packed. Such was the people's eagerness to hear about Jesus.

Almost all those who attended were eager to know Jesus as their Lord and Saviour.

There was such joy on their faces afterwards.

People were so thirsty for the Word of God. Even at 10.30 pm they were asking Peter to preach more. It took nearly an hour to clear the place.

Many sick were healed.

A man testified that his four-year-old deaf and dumb child had heard and spoken for the first time since birth. The blind received their sight and many deaf people were healed.

A woman testified that she could now see clearly without her glasses and many others witnessed to the fact that pains in their backs and joints had instantly gone.

Many others were healed of sicknesses and diseases but, due to the shortage of time, we could not call them all to the stage to testify publicly.

People's faces radiated a joy that they had never known before because Jesus was going to their homes with them.

This was the most remarkable gathering in the history of our town.

Pastor Nazir Masih

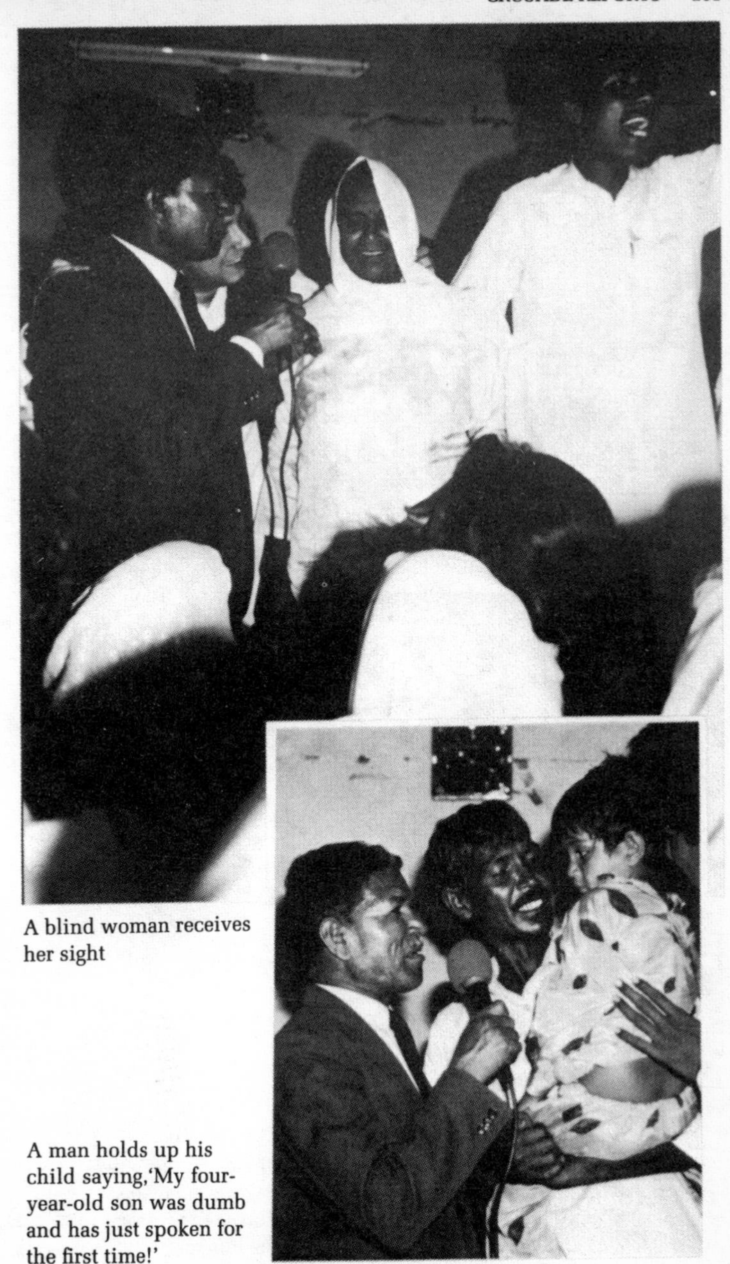

A blind woman receives her sight

A man holds up his child saying,'My four-year-old son was dumb and has just spoken for the first time!'

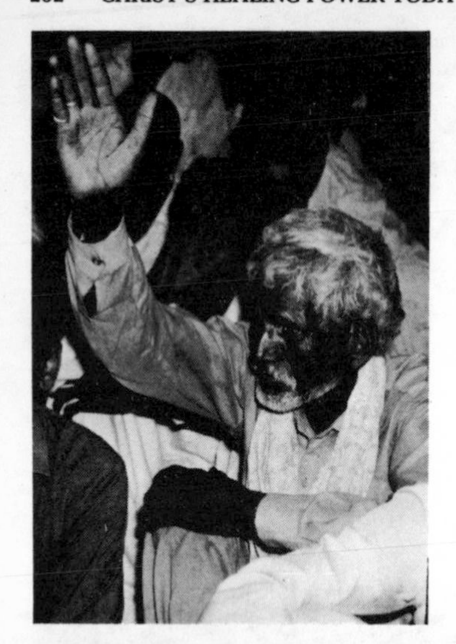

Photos on these two pages were taken during the crusade in the Punjab.

ZIMBABWE – HERE WE COME!

'You must come out to Zimbabwe sometime,' said Dave Prosser, Director of New Life Ministries International, when we met during one of our UK crusades.

About a year later, I was introduced to Ron Davis, Director of Global Literature Lifeline, an organisation pioneering literature and relief work in Zimbabwe and throughout Southern Africa.

'You must come out to Zimbabwe,' Ron commented as we parted company.

God seemed to be speaking.

So, several letters and phone calls later, some friends and I touched down on Zimbabwe soil for fourteen days of non-stop events.

Zimbabwe is a very beautiful country. Many of the streets are lined with purple jacaranda trees and bananas. Pawpaws and passion fruit grow in abundance. One of the most unreal sights as a Westerner is seeing Woolworth's, Barclays Bank and even Wimpy burger bars, just yards away from mud and thatched dwellings.

In my diary I recorded some of the lessons learned afresh during the tour.

God is in Control

What may have naturally appeared to be chance meetings with Dave and Ron was a part of the plan of our sovereign God. He is in control! This was just one of many examples of His ability to 'arrange' meetings. He can make sure that we are in the right place at the right time.

If we want God's will for our lives and are walking in obedience to Him, I believe that it is very hard to miss. So often, initial contacts with people may appear mere co-incidences, but are later revealed to be 'God-incidences'.

> We know that all things work together for good to those who love God and are called according to His purposes.
> Romans 8:28

As we flew over Mozambique's military base later in the trip, and saw the two hundred plus missiles already on their launch pads (five million pound's worth of weapons, while their people are starving!) I thought, 'I am so glad that Jesus is on the throne and ultimately in control.'

We are living in days when people are full of fear. However, it is good to know as believers that we can rest assured in the security that Jesus Christ is Lord!

As we boarded the six-seater Missionary Aviation Fellowship plane for Mozambique, the pilot pointed to the single propeller at the front of the plane and said, 'That is my fan to keep me cool. If it stops watch me sweat!'

God is a God of Miracles

At the Gweru crusade, five deaf mutes from a local deaf and dumb school were totally healed and spoke for the first time. From then onwards they returned every night to learn new words.

By the end of the crusade they could speak more English than the local dialect. Ron later informed us that the boys were being taught Matabili and were among fifty new folk attending one of the participating churches.

As we left Gweru, these five lads waved and shouted in English, 'Bye, bye, Peter.' This was just one of the amazing testimonies to God's power to work miracles today.

The first night of the Hwange Crusade we had to close the meeting because the people at the front of the stadium were getting crushed as the crowd surged forward to see the miracles. During the second night of the crusade a little blind boy received his sight and eleven-year-old Farayi Lumbika who had been deaf from birth in his right ear, was totally healed after prayer. Both were well known by the local people.

How we need to learn from the simple faith of our African brethren and to repent of our unbelief, that we too might see more miracles in our land.

A Mighty Harvest is Waiting to be Reaped

Jesus told us to lift up our eyes and to look, for the fields are already white unto harvest. If the harvest was ready for harvesting then when He spoke those words nearly two thousand years ago, what must they be now? I believe that it is time for us to stop making excuses for not evangelising, to stop listening to the devil's lie that 'we are not ready' and to start obeying Jesus' commission to 'GO' (Matthew 28:19).

In the region of 90% of those who attended the crusades were unsaved, and several hundreds came forward to give their lives to Christ. We have since heard that lots of new converts have been added to the local churches.

At Hwange several thousand people crammed into the open air arena. Each night folk surged forward to receive Christ. This was a super response when you consider that very few people had previously attended churches in the district.

As Ron Davis summed up the trip: 'Heaven is much richer with many coming to Christ. Our time together was a series of events written by the Holy Spirit.'

GOD LOVES BAGUIO CITY

After a twenty-four-hour flight and a seven-hour drive (in a nineteen-year-old van!) I arrived in Baguio, the Philippines' second largest city. Just four hours later I was speaking at the first outreach meeting in Baguio's massive park. Many met with Christ and at one meeting God brought such conviction of sin that every one of the people who came for salvation had tears streaming down their faces as they got right with God.

After this short event, eighty of the ministers from the region extended an invitation for us to return for a major area-wide crusade.

It was exciting as leaders ranging from Anglicans and Pentecostals to Southern Baptists all felt that it was God's timing for Baguio City.

One pastor said, 'God gave me a vision of a man preaching here several months ago. When I saw you I said to my wife, 'That's the man in the vision.' God has sent you to us.'

We had felt it right to hire all of the buses we could to bring people in from all the outlying districts, so that no one could say that they did not have an opportunity to hear the gospel.

It was not until a couple of months after the crusade when an earthquake hit the city and hundreds of lives were lost, that it became evident how perfect God's timing was. For many this was their last opportunity to hear the gospel!

The months of preparation had been worthwhile as all of the churches in the city worked together. It is exciting when churches lay aside their differences and unite for the Kingdom of God. Psalm 133 tells us that it is a sure guarantee of blessing.

The streets were lined with banners, the walls covered in posters and tens of thousands of handbills handed out.

Each night of the crusade people eagerly flocked forward to give their lives to Christ.

Such testimonies were heard as, 'Today is my birthday. This is the most wonderful birthday present I could have received. I was walking though the park and decided to stop and listen. Tonight, I have given my life to Jesus.'

After ministering to those who had come to Christ, I prayed a prayer for healing, from the platform, for those who were sick. The testimonies of those healed were astounding. The first forward was an excited lady and her daughter.

The daughter told how her mother had been blind and as Peter had prayed, God had opened her eyes (photo below). You should have seen the wonderful joy on the faces of her family.

Then a man came forward and testified that he too had been blind and now could see (photo below).

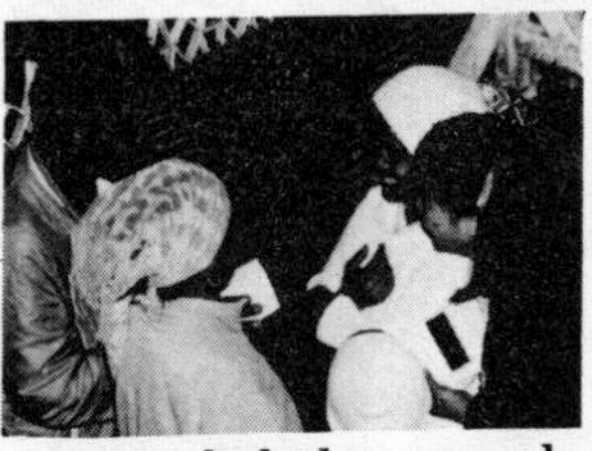

Two blind people completely healed on the first night! The man proceeded to touch my nose and to demonstrate to the audience how God had healed him.

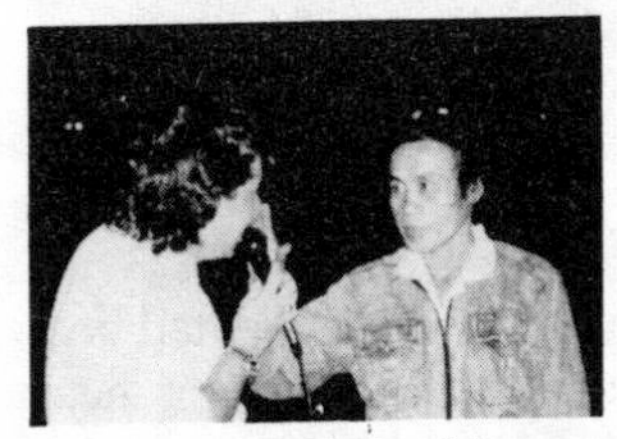

He then attended the crusade each night to find out who this Jesus was who had healed him and on the third night he gave his life to Christ.

A man who had been paralysed for three years was carried to the meeting by two friends (photo opposite).

He stood and walked in Jesus' Name!

MIRACLES IN THE MOUNTAINS

At La Trinadad, Philippines, a man testified that he had been left paralysed down his left-hand side following a heart attack, but was healed as I prayed (photos above).

Several weeks after the crusade, the organisers sent a list of others confirmed healed. Amongst them Diana Bargachon was healed of diabetes and a goitre, Kimberly Kasino was healed of epilepsy and a brain defect and Josefa Teiyabar, a dumb mute had spoken for the first time at the crusade and had continued to speak since that time. A twelve-year-old boy who had been deaf from birth had received his hearing.

Many came forward to receive Christ at the La Trinidad crusade (photo above).

Many other sick people testified to receiving healing including a woman whose hearing in her left ear was completely restored and an old lady, Carol Vallas, who had been blind and whose eyes were opened in Jesus' Name. Those who knew her began to clap and praise the Lord as she copied movements made by people from the other side of the hall. At the close of the meeting, her overjoyed friends had to chase after her as she ran after the bus unaccompanied!

In MANILLA two people who had previously been deaf came forward and testified to being completely healed and that they could now hear perfectly. Many others gave their lives to Christ. One lady came up overjoyed that her husband had attended a Christian meeting for the first time and had been saved.

The Filipinos have been a very hurt and abused people. At one meeting, the Lord laid on my heart a message of healing for the brokenhearted. At the end of the message about three-quarters of the gathering were weeping and hugging as God set them free.

Baguio City, La Trinidad, and Manila were also locations for pastors' conferences.

Most of the pastors have no formal training or access to Christian books. Some do not even have an Old Testament!

the leaders are really hungry for spiritual input. On the Island of Mindanao, one brother whom Reach Out Ministries have been able to help and encourage, has trained ninety-five men who have now planted churches all over the island in towns where there had been no previous evangelical witness.

THE GREATER ONE IS COME!

The message to the Besao tribe in the Philippines was to turn from their animal sacrifices to the true and living God, for the Greater One has come – Jesus!

The first night of the crusade, Luke Matias, the Barangay Captain (district leader) and head of the pagan animal sacrificing, was healed. He had been crippled after falling out of a tree. But in Jesus' Name, he stood straight, completely healed by the power of God. Word soon travelled and the second night of the crusade around half of the town gathered. Luke was one of several hundred who met with Jesus as Saviour. Hundreds of Bibles in the local dialect were also distributed among those who were saved.

Left: Luke Matias, the crippled Besao District leader who was healed and saved during the Besao Crusade. Right: Bibles were distributed in their own dialect.

MANY TURN TO CHRIST AT TADIAN

The Tadian Crusade found Peter and the team in the centre of severe fighting between the Philippine Army and the Communist MPA terrorists, who had set up a stronghold in the town.

Things were so bad, that just days before the crusade began, over 3,000 soldiers had been drafted in. The terrorists had just attacked a convoy, killing the soldiers and so it was quite disconcerting for Peter preaching in the dark, knowing that MPA terrorists and soldiers were present in the meeting and that there were guns everywhere. A curfew had been extended for the crusade, but after 8pm everyone was told that anything seen moving would be shot!

Yet during the crusade hundreds eagerly responded for salvation, on hearing the message of God's love. This is amazing when you realise that according to the organisers, only twenty-five people (including children) had previously attended a church. We were later informed that many of the military men met with Christ.

Many respond at Tadian to receive Christ.

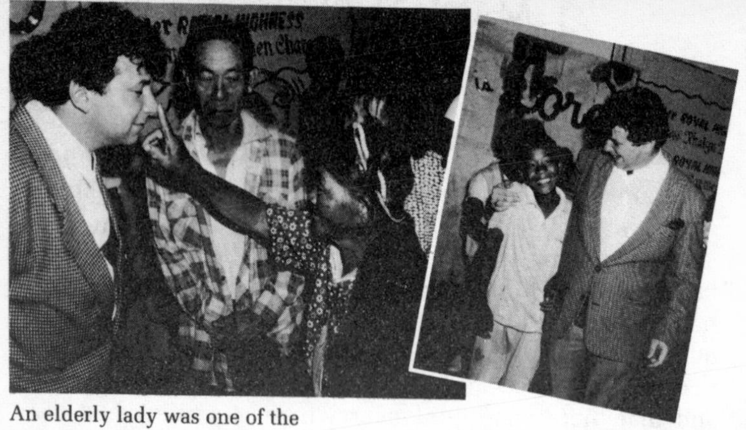

An elderly lady was one of the many to receive her sight.

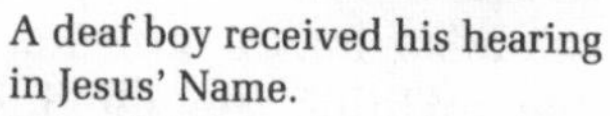

A deaf boy received his hearing in Jesus' Name.

Many crippled people walked.

A trible man's right eye was healed.

Christina Agogor had no sense of smell and was healed in Jesus' Name. She smelt perfume for the first time. Her friend whom the team had unsuccessfully witnessed to earlier, said, 'Now I believe. I was at college with Christina and knew that she had no sense of smell. Now I know that what you have said is true.'

PASTORS GATHER IN COMMUNIST MOZAMBIQUE

Mozambique has been a hard country to gain entry to. Most of the missionaries were expelled following the so-called 'Independence' in 1975. 'Independence' was a Marxist take-over and the start of years of terrible persecution for believers, with many church leaders being imprisoned and church buildings seized and destroyed.

Poverty now grips this once fertile and prosperous country, which is rich in mineral deposits. During our 1983 visit, there was no food or drink on sale in shops and even bread had been unavailable for three weeks. One positive outcome of the economic collapse however, has been that Mozambique has had to open its borders once again to the outside world.

I was invited to speak at a Leaders Conference for 400 pastors who had got together for the first time since the take-over, a unique event for a Marxist country. The conference drew together ministers from extremely varied backgrounds and denominations.

Although the event was arranged for pastors, the people soon found out about it and sneaked in the unsaved and sick, many of whom met with Christ and were healed. One over-joyed woman testified publicly of how she had brought along her dumb daughter, who spoke for the first time.

Some of the pastors who attended the conference.

REACHING OUT IN DENMARK

Since 1980 we have had an increasing ministry input into Denmark and I have become a close friend of leaders right across the denominational scene.

Denmark has had the lowest weekly church attendance in Europe and the highest number of self-declared atheists. But, a breakthrough is coming! After one recent tour Per Eivind Stig, the Director of Youth With A Mission, Denmark, wrote:

The flames of excitement have begun to spread and we have received many good reports from across Denmark. People are becoming bold in reaching out and they have been sharing what the Lord has done. We are so grateful to the Lord for leading you to minister together with us here.

Thomas Brandt recently accompanied me on a four-part tour of the country covering a total of forty different venues. He wrote:

A lot of us Danes were inspired that God is actually working today. Of course we knew it with our heads, but not always in our hearts. What we saw and heard as you shared, gave us a new faith in the Lord. Lots of people, even in some of the very conservative congregations, dedicated their lives to the Lord afresh. A lot of people also came forward to receive Jesus as their Saviour.

On one of the nights a man attended who had not been along to a church service since childhood. He was a real masculine, 'Viking' type, and had seen a poster advertising the meeting in his local bank. He came along and received Christ.

I've Been Healed!

Edith Vestergaard

Because of arthritis, the use of my left arm had greatly deteriorated. I have hardly been able to use it for ten years. I could not move it out sideways or lift it from my body.

It was so painful that I could not even close the door. But when Peter prayed for me, I was completely healed. My son's left knee was also completely healed too.

So Have I!

John Christensen

My back was healed last year when Peter visited our church. I am a bricklayer and have suffered from backpains for three years. I would have to lay down on the floor in pain after work.

Peter called me forward with a word of knowledge that explained my pain exactly. I went forward and God healed me. I have felt no pain since and am working hard bricklaying.

AN OUTPOURING IN BRITAIN

There was a mighty outpouring of the Holy Spirit at a summer camp in England where Peter spoke on the subject of 'The Holy Spirit's Power and Gifts Today'.

Many were saved in the meetings and others re-dedicated their lives to Christ.

'Raise your hands if you were healed in yesterday's meeting, when I spoke on "Miracles, Healing and Faith",' Peter asked. 'Not if you have received it by faith and hope to see the results later, but you were actually physically healed in the meeting.'

Of the 2,000 people present, over 500 raised their hands to say that they had been healed in that one meeting, in England! (Photo below.)

One visitor who had missed the previous day's meeting exclaimed, 'I couldn't believe it. I seemed to be the only person without my hand up!'

As Peter preached the Word, people were healed all over the vast hall. Many testified that they had never seen such miracles and blessings in Britain before.

Many deaf people testified that their hearing had been healed.

SOME EXCERPTS FROM REACH OUT MINISTRIES' RECENT UK MAIL

I have had very bad arthritis of the knees, shoulder and back for the past twenty years. I asked Peter to offer a prayer, not for the Lord to cure me, but to stop it getting worse. But, the Lord completely healed me. I have given my distalgesics to my cousin! C.A.

If it wasn't for you, I would still be an old backslider. I backslid for thirty years and have come back into His fold. I thank Him for taking me back after all those long years of ignoring Him. He has been wonderful to me. S.L. aged 64

I feel completely reborn. I know that God has forgiven me. M.C.

Though my parents are missionaries, I had never given my life to Christ. I was saved the first night that you spoke. D.B.

I feel so different now, so much closer to God and to my wife. We have fallen in love all over again. P.H.

Many others were saved and healed during the UK tour meetings.

One of the highlights was a rally in Wells Cathedral where seventy-six people came forward at the close of the message to make a commitment of their lives to Christ. The whole place was filled with excitement and praise. The only complaint was from a verger because the place was so packed that the fire exit points were blocked!

In Chelmsford on another night, the power of the Lord was so present, that a married couple who had not been in the meeting, walked into the building afterwards as they were so aware of the presence of God. In seconds, with tears running down their faces, they both received Christ.

One pastor wrote:

Many people have confirmed that they were healed during your recent tour meeting. One man who had cancer has since had further tests which show no trace remaining. We give thanks to God for these miracles and for the many who became Christians. Several were baptised this Sunday.

Testimonies were received from others saying:

We brought our baby to your meeting. He was totally deaf and the Lord completely healed him. He can hear perfectly now.

My mother has just got saved.

My husband has become a Christian. For many years I have been praying for him.

In the past I have done a lot of stupid things and could not forgive myself. On Thursday night you prayed for me. I can say I physically felt the guilt leave and God's forgiveness and love enter. Now I have Jesus. The meeting was amazing, we were able to see God move in such a powerful way, an experience we never had before.

At a meeting in Somerset, the Holy Spirit so fell on those who came for prayer, that there was hardly a dry eye in the place. Someone asked Peter if he had shares in Kleenex tissues!

One man wrote saying:

A party of sixty of us came to your Crusade on Tuesday night. Apart from the few who were already Christians, there was a 100% conversion rate. Praise the Lord! It looks to me as if our college is having a spiritual revival. The change here is fantastic, and our prayer groups have swelled in numbers, which is a great thing to witness. We still remember you in our prayers here and trust that your marvellous work will continue to grow.

Please Pray for the Ongoing Worldwide Crusades of REACH OUT MINISTRIES.

APPENDIX 1

REACHING THE MASSES

Through mass evangelism millions of lives have been touched and hundreds of thousands brought to faith in Jesus Christ. There is certainly a biblical precedent for mass evangelism. Three thousand were saved in one public rally on the day of Pentecost. Acts chapter 8 records the account of a whole city turning to Christ as a result of Philip's ministry. We see the example in Jesus' ministry too, which combined addressing the crowds and personal witness to individuals. Both are necessary and complementary.

Let us consider some reasons why mass evangelism is as vital today as ever.

1 Mass Evangelistic Crusades Reach Thousands for Christ

Despite criticism levelled at this method by some, mass crusades are behind the phenomenal church growth in Africa, Asia and South America. The current migration from rural to urban areas is bringing thousands to our major towns and cities and they need to be reached.

2 Mass Crusades Often See the Reaping of Seed Already Sown

Such events give believers an unique opportunity to bring friends under the sound of the gospel.

3 Christians Often Catch a Vision to Reach Out to the Lost as a Result of Mass Evangelistic Crusades

Seeing evangelists in action in large cities has inspired hundreds of others to evangelise smaller towns and villages. At least four of my interpreters in Africa are now national evangelists, drawing thousands to their own meetings.

4 Many Believers Receive a Call to the Ministry as a Result of Evangelistic Crusades

5 Many Backsliders Come Back to Christ at Such Events and Others are Stirred to a New Dedication

6 Such Events Help Believers Present a United Front to the World

Jesus said when the world sees that we are one they will believe.

7 Such Events Attract Young People who have been Largely Indifferent to much Local Church Evangelism

8 God's Spirit Often Comes Down in Power

Mighty signs and wonders regularly accompany such events. Whilst, for example, I do not major on healing and miracles at our crusades, God still confirms His Word with signs following, as promised in His Word. (Mark 16:20, Acts 14:3, John 6:2, John 2:23, Acts 8:6, Acts 9:32–35 and Hebrews 13:8).

9 Such Events can Stir a Locality

Large crusades are not easy to ignore. Conversations everywhere, on the streets, in restaurants and homes, revolve around the Lord. There is a sense of expectancy in the air. People become inquisitive. Questions are raised about all aspects of life and Bibles are often sold in great numbers.

10 Such Events Can Place the Media at our Disposal

Newspapers, radio and TV reports can bring something of the good news to those who would not venture near a Christian meeting.

11 Crusades Stir Believers to Prayer

Any event that causes Christians to gather and unite in faith-filled, fervent prayer must be good. Such commitment to prayer usually continues long after a crusade has finished.

12 Such Events can be a Real Encouragement to Isolated Believers in Rural Villages

Being among a crowd of believers can inspire new confidence and bring a real sense of belonging.

13 Mass Evangelistic Crusades Provide an Opportunity for Many Christians to Lead Someone Else to Christ

Many believers have never had the experience of leading someone else to Christ. Seeing how open people can be to the gospel and how easy it is to bring another to the Lord, can release timid believers and be the beginning of an ongoing, effective witness.

14 Such Events can Reach Thousands who Might Not Otherwise Hear the Gospel

If we are to win the world only by friendship evangelism, we will need to win something like 17,777 each! How we need those with a gift for reaching thousands at a time.

In 110 cities of our world, there is just one missionary working to one million people!

80,000 people pass into a Christless eternity every day, many never having heard the gospel once!

Although the whole body of Christ ought to be faithfully witnessing, let us not deceive ourselves that this is always so.

The harvest is truly vast and the labourers few. Let us join together to see a mighty reaping for Jesus in the days ahead.

APPENDIX 2

INSIGHT

An interview with Peter Gammons extracted from *Abundant Life Magazine*. (Used with permission.)

How did you become a Christian?

I was searching for answers to life and began to get involved with the music business, because I thought that was the route to happiness. I had a lot of questions and one day I had an invitation to go to hear an evangelist. I put it off for a long while, but eventually decided to go. I got saved that same night. It was the first time I remember ever hearing the gospel.

When were you filled with the Holy Spirit?

Just over a year later. I was so excited having met with the Lord, that I wanted to tell the world, but they didn't seem very interested. The more I read the Bible, the more I realised that the people I was reading about had something that I hadn't got. So I went to a meeting, determined to go forward, (I hadn't been to one where they gave the opportunity to respond, but I knew that they would at this one). I decided that I would go for whatever they invited people forward for. The man said 'What have you come for?' I said 'I don't know, but I want something.' He said, 'Have you been baptised in the Spirit?' I replied, 'I've never heard of it.' So he prayed for me and I received. It made an amazing difference. Within three days I led my first soul to Christ and within the next three days that person led someone else to Christ. So in six days I was a 'grandad'. I soon realised that God had called me to be an evangelist.

What was the biggest breakthrough that you've had in your ministry?

Back in 1977, I was at a meeting held in a barn, on a farm near St Ives in Cambridgeshire. Before the meeting began, a woman approached me and said questioningly, 'Peter?' 'Yes', I replied, 'do I know you?' 'No', she answered. 'I was sitting at home, when the Lord told me to come here and that He would show me who 'Peter' was and that I had to give you a message, that you will take His healing message and power to the world.' 'Were you coming to the meeting?' I asked, somewhat shocked at her words. 'No', she replied, 'I live seven miles away, so I had to call a taxi to bring me here. The taxi is waiting for me outside so I can leave.' With that she left.

The meeting began and I was sitting in the middle of the 200–300 people who had attended. Suddenly, in the middle of all singing together the hymn, 'To God be the Glory', the preacher, Edgar Webb, whom I had never seen or even heard of before, said loudly, 'Stop!' Then, pointing at me, he said, 'You boy, come here.'

I was terrified. Friends said I went white as I walked to the front, wondering what God had told him! I thought, 'Lord, have I done something wrong?'

As I arrived at the front, Edgar began to prophecy how the power of God would come upon me and how I would minister in the power of the Holy Spirit. The anointing of the Holy Spirit came upon me and I went down under the overwhelming presence of the Lord.[1] I arose knowing that God had done something. I later discovered that Edgar had received this mighty anointing under the ministry of Kathryn Kuhlman and now felt that he was passing on the anointing to me.

At the close of the meeting, an extremely fat man came up to me, saying, 'Pray for me that I might be filled with the Holy Spirit.' I looked around for Edgar, but the man said, 'Not him, you. You got the prophecy.' As I touched him, he went down under the power of the Holy Spirit and because he was so big, knocked everyone flying around him!

From that day, more and more invitations came in and soon I could not fulfil the invitations that were coming in for ministry and continue a full-time job.

What is your call?

The Word of the Lord was to 'take Christ's healing message and power to the world'. God cares. He wants to heal our hurting world – body, soul and spirit. That is why the message I share is of wholeness in Christ.

To the paralytic, He not only said, 'Your sins are forgiven', but, 'Arise, take up your bed and walk.' That is healing for the whole person. This is the 'gospel', the good news that Jesus told us to take to every creature (Mark 16:15–20).

Where was your first overseas mission?

Tanzania. There was a missionary who was returning to England after a number of years in Tanzania and he asked me to join him to hold the last meetings. God did some great things there and I was invited back and returned for several crusades. That's the way it works. I go somewhere for a crusade and there always seems to be someone there, in the congregation, who is the next contact and who says, 'Will you come to us next?' God opens the next door through that person and then He makes an appointment with someone else to be at that event.

What's your favourite memory from any crusade?

There are so many. It's always a great thrill when you see tens of thousands of unbelievers in the meeting. There is no greater thrill than seeing people come to Christ.

I think one of my greatest memories is of a crusade in Zimbabwe where five deaf and dumb boys, from a special school, were brought to the meeting. They heard and spoke in Jesus' Name.

The next day a pastor came up to me and said that they hadn't been healed. 'I keep asking them questions and they just look at me blankly' he said. I replied with a smile, 'They don't understand you; they're like babies; they don't know what you're saying as they've never heard before. You've now got to teach them like babies.' So this pastor took these five boys and taught them to speak Matabili.

As we left the city they were speaking more English than they could the local dialect! They were waving and saying, 'Bye-bye Peter!' The next time I went back, the pastor had been training them for just over a year. It was really an amazing miracle.

You were a minister in a large Baptist church. What made you give up that ministry?

Both the call of God and the challenge of the unreached. I was faced with the challenge of how I could preach to my church week by week, to folk who knew and loved the Lord, when over half the world had never heard the gospel. 2.2 billion of the world's population have never heard the saving message of Jesus. Every day 80,000 people die and enter a Christless eternity.

I knew that I had to go.

It is a challenge that every Christian and every church should face. What are we doing to reach the unreached peoples of our world? It is not enough to just reach out in our own towns. Jesus did not tell us to just go to Jerusalem, but also to the ends of the earth!

I am still sent out from the church where I was a minister and praise God for a good home base. All of our team members are church-based and sent out with the blessing of their local churches.

Do you speak many different languages?

I know how to say 'Hello' in lots of languages but that's about it. They say that if you speak three languages you're trilingual, if you speak two languages you're bilingual and if you speak one language you're English!

What's the funniest thing that has ever happened to you?

I was working on one of my books in a London hotel and started to run the bath. I ran the hot water first in case it ran out, thinking that I could add cold water later. While it was running I got engrossed in my book and forgot about the bath. Suddenly I thought 'Bath!' and ran into the bathroom. By now the water was coming into the bedroom! It was boiling hot too and I had no clothes on at the time so I was shouting 'Argh!' and hopping about as the water was burning my feet. At that point the door was flung open and in came the Manager and a woman assistant. I grabbed my shirt and held it in front of me. They asked me what I was doing and I said, 'Uh, I'm having a bath.' They said, 'You're flooding the hotel. We've had to close the room below and the restaurant below that!' That was very embarrassing; even more so as they had given me a special rate to stay there. I've never dared go back!

What's your advice to budding, eager missionaries?

Get around anointed preachers, where people get saved and where the sick are healed. Learn, watch, and step out in faith too. That is how I was trained and I praise God for it.

I used to travel long distances, back in the early days, to hear anointed ministries. Being around Holy Spirit empowered ministries is the best training for someone called to be an evangelist. This is how Jesus trained His disciples; they worked with Him and caught the vision, caught the message and caught the anointing. That is why I believe the Lord has led us to start the 'School of Evangelism and World Mission', to equip and mobilise workers in the power of the Spirit.

Do you always organise your crusades from here or are they organised for you and you just go and speak?

I usually have a co-ordinator at the place we are going to. We give them clear guidelines for setting up the crusade and keep checking at various points during the build-up as to how things are progressing. In each country where I work, there is one main co-ordinator who organises and oversees the events.

Thousands respond to receive Christ in your crusades. What do you do about follow-up?

We only work in conjunction with churches and missionaries who will commit themselves to caring for the fruit of the crusades. A large team of counsellors are trained prior to the event and one of their jobs is to take down the names and addresses of all those counselled. The follow-up team is then expected to visit them within forty-eight hours of their response. All the cards are passed to ministers and pastors who are committed to the crusade. This works well. We have a high percentage who respond in our crusades who are still part of a local church a year later. In at least one place 100% of those who responded were active in the local churches a year later. Our target is always 100%.

Note

[1] See Peter's book, *A Touch from Heaven.*

APPENDIX 3

MIRACLES IN THE BOOK OF ACTS

1:3	Jesus presents Himself alive by many infallible proofs.
1:9–11	The Lord's ascension and a visitation of angelic messengers.
2:1–41	The promised Holy Spirit comes and visitors from all over hear the disciples speak in their own languages, ending in three thousand being converted.
2:43,47	God grants signs and wonders and adds daily to the church.
3:1 – 4:22	A lame man is healed and enters the temple, walking, leaping and praising God, giving Peter an opportunity to preach and resulting in thousands more being converted.
4:23–33	As the believers meet to praise, to pray for boldness and for God to stretch out His hand to heal, the building is shaken and those assembled are all filled afresh with the Holy Spirit.
5:1–11	Ananias and Sapphira are supernaturally judged.
5:12–16	Many more signs and wonders are done among the people and multitudes added to the church.
5:17–25	The angered Sadducees and high priests imprison the apostles, but an angel releases them.
6:8	Signs and wonders follow Stephen's ministry.
7:54–60	The Lord appears as Stephen is about to be stoned.
8:4–25	Hearing Philip's message and seeing the miracles, including the lame and paralysed being healed, a mighty revival breaks out in Samaria, where many are saved and filled with the Holy Spirit.
8:26–40	Philip is directed by an angel to encounter a key

Ethiopian official and then is supernaturally transported to his next mission.

9:1–9 Saul of Tarsus has a dramatic encounter with the Lord on the way to Damascus.

9:10–19 A devout disciple called Ananias is told in a vision where Saul is staying and sent to lay hands on him that he might receive his sight and be filled with the Holy Spirit.

9:32–35 After being paralysed and bedridden for eight years, Aeneas is healed, resulting in all the people of Lydda and Sharon turning to the Lord.

9:36–43 Tabitha is raised from the dead, resulting in many at Joppa believing.

10:1 – 11:18 Cornelius, his family and friends are all saved and filled with the Holy Spirit after he had received an angelic visitation and Peter a heavenly vision.

11:27–30 After Agabus prophesied concerning an imminent famine, Barnabas and Saul are sent with relief supplies to the brethren in Judea.

12:5–19 Peter imprisoned and bound with chains between two soldiers, is miraculously delivered by an angel, causing no small stir!

12:20–24 Herod is struck down dead by an angel of the Lord.

13:1–4 Via the prophetic word, Barnabas and Saul are set apart for further ministry.

13:4–12 A sorcerer is blinded for seeking to turn the Proconsul, Sergius Paulas, away from the faith, resulting in the official's conversion.

14:1–3 At Iconium the Lord bore witness to Paul and Barnabas' words, granting signs and wonders and a great multitude of Jews and Greeks believed.

14:8–10 A man at Lystra who had been crippled from birth and had never walked is raised up.

14:19–20 Paul is stoned and left for dead, but is miraculously raised up and the next day continues his missionary journey.

16:6–10 Paul is supernaturally directed in ministry by the Lord.

16:16–19 A fortune-teller is delivered from her demonic bondages, leading to Paul and Silas being imprisoned.

16:25–34	The jailer and his family are all saved, after the doors are miraculously opened and their chains fall off.
18:9,10	The Lord speaks to Paul in a vision and tells him to stay in Corinth.
19:1–6	The believers at Ephesus are filled with the Holy Spirit, speak in tongues and prophesy.
19:11,12	People are healed and set free when Paul's handkerchiefs are taken to them.
19:13–20	Counterfeit ministries are exposed and many more turn to Christ and renounce their past occult practices.
20:7–12	A young man called Eutychus, who had died after falling asleep during Paul's sermon and falling out of a third storey window, is raised back to life.
21:10–11	Agabus prophesies.
23:11	The Lord appears to Paul and encourages him.
27:23–25	Paul receives an angelic visitation.
28:1–6	Paul is bitten by a poisonous snake but is unharmed.
28:7,8	The father of a leading citizen is healed of a fever and dysentery.
28:9	All the other sick on the island came and were healed.

Conclusion

The Book of Acts has never finished. God wants your life to be Acts chapter 29!

> 'Grant to your servants that with all boldness they may speak Your word, by stretching out Your hand to heal, and that signs and wonders may be done through the Name of Your holy Servant Jesus.' Acts 4:29,30

APPENDIX 4

CHURCH GROWTH AND MIRACLES IN THE BOOK OF ACTS

A study of church growth in the Book of Acts demonstrates the important connection between signs and wonders and the preached Word.

Signs and Wonders	Preaching	Church Growth
2:1–13	2:14–36	2:37–41
2:43	2:42	2:47
3:1–11	3:12 – 4:3	4:4
5:12–13		5:14
8:6	8:6	8:12
8:26–29	8:35	8:38
9:1–5		9:6
9:32–34		
9:36–41		9:42
10:3,10,44	10:34–43	10:47
13:1–3		Churches planted in Europe and Asia
13:6–11		13:12
14:3	14:1–3	14:4
14:8–10	14:15–18	14:19–22
16:8–10		European churches planted
19:11–15	19:10	19:18
28:8,9		Church started here according to some church historians.

APPENDIX 5

THE GOSPEL ACCOUNTS OF JESUS' HEALING MINISTRY

	Matthew	Mark	Luke	John
Many around Galilee are healed & set free, including epileptics and paralytics	4:23–25			
A demoniac is set free at Capernaum		1:21–28	4:31–37	
Peter's mother-in-law is healed	8:14,15	1:29–31	4:38,39	
Many are healed and delivered at Capernaum	8:16	1:32,34	4:40,41	
Jesus heals a leper	8:1–4	1:40–45	5:12–16	
Jesus heals a paralytic	9:1–8	2:1–12	5:17–26	
Many are healed as Jesus toured the cities and villages	9:35			
A man's withered hand is healed	12:9–14	3:1–6	6:6–11	
Multitudes are healed and set free	12:14,15	3:7–12	6:17–19	
A nobleman's son is healed				4:46–54
A centurion's servant is healed	8:5–13		7:1–10	

	Matthew	Mark	Luke	John
A widow's son is raised from the dead			7:11–17	
Many are healed of infirmities, afflictions, blindness and are set free			7:21	
Mary Magdalene and other women are delivered			8:2,3	
The Gadarene demoniac is set free	8:28–34	5:1–20	8:26–39	
Jairus' daughter is raised from the dead and a woman with a haemorrhage is healed	9:18–26	5:21–43	8:40–56	
Two blind men have their sight restored	9:27–31			
A mute demoniac is healed	9:32–34			
A blind and dumb man is healed	12:22		11:14	
Jesus healed the sick from a crowd that followed him	14:14		9:11	6:2
Jesus has compassion on the multitudes and heals their sick	14:14			
Only a few sick folk are healed at Nazareth because of their unbelief	13:58	6:5,6		
Multitudes more at Gennesaret are healed. As many as touched Him are made whole	14:34–36	6:53–56		

	Matthew	Mark	Luke	John
A Gentile woman's daughter is delivered	15:21–28	7:24–30		
A deaf and dumb man is healed		7:32–37		
Many lame, blind, dumb and maimed are healed at Decapolis	15:29–31			
A blind man is healed		8:22–26		
An epileptic boy is healed	17:14–21	9:17–29	9:38–42	
A man who had been blind from birth is healed at Jerusalem				9:1–41
A multitude follow Jesus and are healed	19:2			
Blind and lame people are healed	21:14			
A crippled woman is healed			13:10–17	
A man is healed of dropsy			14:1–6	
Lazarus is raised from the dead				11:1–44
Ten lepers are healed			17:11–19	
Blind Bartimaeus is healed		10:46–52	18:35–43	
Malchus' ear is restored			22:50,51	

APPENDIX 6

OLD TESTAMENT REFERENCES TO HEALING

Genesis
- 18:10–14
- 20:17
- 21:1–3
- 29:31

Exodus
- 15:26
- 23:25

Numbers
- 12:1–15
- 16:41–50
- 21:4–9

Deuteronomy
- 7:12–15

1 Samuel
- 1:10–20

1 Kings
- 17:17–24

2 Kings
- 4:8–37
- 5:1–14
- 13:21
- 20:1–11

Nehemiah
- 9:21

Job
- 42:10

Psalms
- 30:2
- 103:1–3
- 107:17–20

Isaiah
- 33:20–24
- 35:5,6
- 38:1–5
- 53:3–5
- 58:6–9
- 61:1–3

Daniel
- 4:28–37

Hosea
- 6:1

Malachi
- 4:2

Let's keep in touch!

Reach Out Magazine is the official publication of Reach Out Ministries and is sent out on request to keep the friends and supporters of Peter Gammons up-to-date with news, current prayer topics and details of forthcoming events.

A current catalogue of cassettes, videos and other books by Peter Gammons is also available on request.

Write for More Details To:
Reach Out Ministries
PO BOX 130
Walton on Thames
Surrey
KT12 2RU
England

Please Add My Name to your Mailing List to Receive 'Reach Out Magazine'.

NAME: ______________________________

ADDRESS: ______________________________

____

____________ POSTCODE: ____________

RETURN TO:

Reach Out Ministries (HQ), PO BOX 130, Walton on Thames, Surrey KT12 2RU, England

Reach Out Ministries USA, PO BOX 276, Pompton Plains, NJ 07444, USA

Reach Out Ministries Scandinavia, PO BOX 155, 8900 Randers, Denmark

Reach Out Ministries Switzerland, POSTFACH 54, CH 9428, Walzenhausen, Switzerland

Peter Gammons is International Director of Reach Out Ministries, who are involved in reaching thousands for Christ through city-wide crusades and outreach events around the world.

REACH OUT MAGAZINE

Reach Out Magazine is sent out on request and contains news, photographs, reports, details of forthcoming meetings and a current message from Peter Gammons.

TAPES

Audio cassettes and videos are available for purchase on a wide range of subjects. These are ideal for use in homes, Bible studies and small group meetings. A current catalogue is available on request.

PUBLICATIONS

Peter is the author of several other books and booklets, including the popular Christian paperbacks, *Battle Stations* and *Believing is Seeing*.

BIBLE COLLEGE

Reach Out Ministries 'School of Evangelism and World Mission', 'School of Leadership' and 'School of Biblical Studies' are run for those feeling God's call on their lives and to equip believers to minister in the power of the Holy Spirit.

CELEBRATION CAMP

Celebration Camp is Reach Out Ministries' major annual UK event, drawing Christians together from right across the Body of Christ for a week of worship, teaching and fellowship. Write for further details concerning Reach Out Ministries' future Conferences and Summer Camps.

SUPPORT

Reach Out Ministries are involved in an all-year-round programme of Crusades and evangelistic events, targeting the unreached of the World. It is a faith venture, supported entirely by the gifts of God's people. Please pray about how you can help to continue and advance this work.

I would like further information on:

____

NAME: ________________________________

ADDRESS: ________________________________

______________ POSTCODE: ______________

Return To:

Reach Out Ministries, PO BOX 130, Walton on Thames, Surrey KT12 2RU, England

ABOUT THE AUTHOR

PETER GAMMONS is an evangelist and Bible teacher. He is also a much sought-after convention speaker.

Peter heads up Reach Out Ministries who are involved in evangelism, leadership training and relief work worldwide.

Jesus said that 'the harvest is vast and the labourers few' (Matthew 9:37). For the past two decades, Peter's life has been committed to harvesting souls on the unreached mission fields of the world, where crowds of up to 60,000 a night attend his crusades.

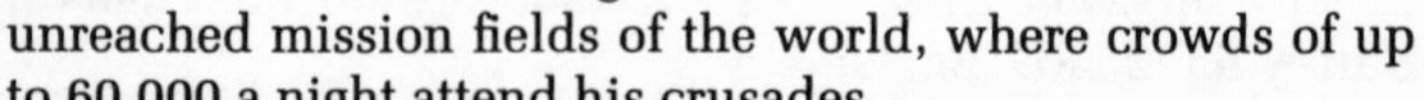

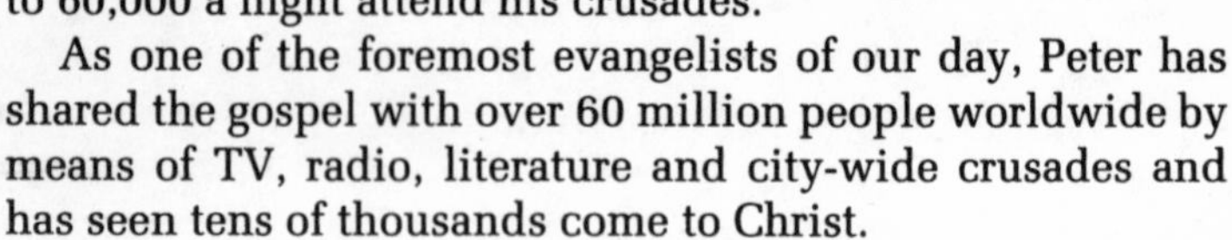

As one of the foremost evangelists of our day, Peter has shared the gospel with over 60 million people worldwide by means of TV, radio, literature and city-wide crusades and has seen tens of thousands come to Christ.

He is also widely used in the gifts of the Holy Spirit, especially words of knowledge and healing. Secular newspapers have carried accounts of people healed in Peter's crusades, including those considered incurable.

He is the author of several popular paperbacks, including *Battle Stations* and *Believing is Seeing*. His books have also been translated into several other languages.

He works closely with leaders right across the denominational scene and is a former pastor of a large Baptist Church in South-West London, where his ministry is still based.